GOOD • OLD • DAYS®

Making
Our Own
Fun
In the Good Old Days®

© *Sweet Victory* by Jim Daly

Edited by Ken and Janice Tate

HOUSE of
WHITE
BIRCHES
PUBLISHERS
SINCE 1947

Making Our Own Fun in the Good Old Days™

Editors: Ken and Janice Tate
Managing Editor: Barb Sprunger
Editorial Assistant: Joanne Neuenschwander
Copy Editors: Conor Allen, Michelle Beck, Nicki Lehman, Läna Schurb
Assistant Editors: Marla Freeman, Marj Morgan, June Sprunger

Publishing Services Manager: Brenda Gallmeyer
Graphic Arts Supervisor: Ronda Bechinski
Cover Design: Erin Augsburger
Production Artists: Erin Augsburger, Pam Gregory
Traffic Coordinator: Sandra Beres
Production Assistants: Cheryl Kempf, Jessica Tate
Photography: Tammy Christian, Christena Green, Kelly Wiard
Photography Stylist: Tammy Nussbaum

Chief Executive Officer: John Robinson
Publishing Director: David McKee
Marketing Director: Shirrel Rhoades
Book Marketing Director: Craig Scott
Editorial Director: Vivian Rothe

Printed in the United States of America
First Printing: 2004
Library of Congress Number: 2004105972
ISBN: 1-59217-049-8
Good Old Days Customer Service: (800) 829-5865

Every effort has been made to ensure the accuracy of the material in this book.
However, the publisher is not responsible for research errors or typographical mistakes in this publication.

We would like to thank the following for the art prints used in this book.

For fine-art prints and more information on the artists featured in *Making Our Own Fun in the Good Old Days*, contact:

Apple Creek Publishing, Hiawatha, IA 52233, (800) 662-1707, www.applecreekpub.com
Curtis Publishing, Indianapolis, IN 46202, (317) 633-2070, www.curtispublishing.com
Jim Daly, P.O. Box 25146, Eugene, OR 97402, www.jimdalyart.com
Newmark USA, Louisville, KY 40299, (502) 266-6752, www.newmarkusa.com
Wild Wings Inc., Lake City, MN 55041, (800) 445-4833, www.wildwings.com

1 2 3 4 5 6 7 8 9

Dear Friends of the Good Old Days,

Janice and I sat on a park bench on the village square of our county seat a couple of years back. It was a summer day, wonderfully hot in fact. We had been shopping and stopped for an ice cream cone under verdant maples that provided shady relief from the afternoon sun.

When we were youngsters we had both spent our share of hours around the square, playing safely while our parents shopped when the downtown was about all the town there was. We played on the old bandstand with friends, roamed sidewalks that converged at the courthouse, or took in the matinee at the Lyric Theatre on the north side of the square.

Drop the Hanky by Hal Sutherland, courtesy of Wild Wings Inc.

As we sat there, trying to make sure that melted ice cream didn't make its way to our wrists, we were struck with the absence of children. In our day, "young'uns"—as we were called—were everywhere. The air pealed with our laughter; the yells of boys and squeals of girls spiced the center of town and made it—well—*alive.*

I wondered aloud at the too-tranquil scene. Janice said she figured that kids were at home in air-conditioned isolation. Surrounded with television, computers and video games, they obviously had no reason to come out and play. Our conversation turned to how we made our own fun back in the Good Old Days. That was the genesis of this book, old playmates reminiscing about youth and all of the good times ready for reaping. It was easy for us to remember the ways we created fun.

First, we were never bored. It seemed we never lacked for something to do. I can remember but once uttering those famous last words: "I'm bored!" I swore I'd never let *that* happen again. There was always fun out there for kids with fertile minds.

The games we played were simple and needed little technology. Whether it was a group game like Red Rover, or mumblety peg with your best friend, our games pulled us together instead of the joystick-pounding isolation of today's video games.

We made our own fun on a shoestring. With little money, we learned how to salvage good times from the recycle bin. I think the most fun I ever had was discovering how to make games out of an old stick, a ball of string or a recycled Montgomery Ward catalog.

When it came to toys, our favorite things were the few store-bought ones we had, simple but sturdy. A favorite doll, sled or yo-yo—toys we had held special places in the hearts of children who had so few. We didn't have toy boxes; we didn't have enough toys to warrant that.

Radio, movies and—later—television provided us sporadic glimpses of a world away from our neck of the woods. There was enough for us to develop heroes and heroines from Tom Mix to Shirley Temple, but not so much that it killed the magic of the moment. Now *that's* entertainment!

Janice and I left the park bench that day knowing we wanted to share this collection of memories with you. Neither heat nor cold could keep us from enjoying life and the wonder of youth. Lack of money never meant lack of adventure. So join us as we remember the Good Old Days when we made our own fun.

Ken Tate

❧ Contents ❧

We Were Never Bored • 6

The Games We Played • 42

Fun on a Shoestring • 72

Our Favorite Things • 104

Now *That's* Entertainment! • 132

We Were Never Bored

Chapter One

Back in the Good Old Days, we were never bored. I'm sure those of younger generations cannot fathom that statement. After all, the modern accoutrements of boredom prevention—television, video games, computers and the like—were at best Flash Gordon serial dreams. No, we were never bored for two very simple reasons.

First, boredom was not *allowed*. I didn't have to utter the words, "Mama, I'm bored." All I had to do was *look* bored and she or Daddy had a sure cure for the affliction. In growing season, garden rows could always be weeded, hoed or cultivated. Mama and Daddy didn't have insecticide, but they sure had bug killers—namely Dennis, Kenny and Donna—and there was no more hated task than plant by plant examinations for potato bugs or tomato worms. In fall or winter there were always leaves to be raked, kindling to be split or wood to be stacked for cold days ahead. I think you get the picture. It is amazing what a strong deterrent hard work is to boredom.

The second reason we were never bored is because we *chose* not to be. It just was no fun at all. We had few toys, but we made our own out of great imaginations. I never had a Lionel play train, but one of my favorite toys was the real railroad track that ran south out of Hollister, Mo., through the valleys along Turkey Creek not far from my childhood home.

I walked almost every mile between Hollister and the Arkansas state line. I walked the rails like a balance beam, seeing how far I could walk without slipping off and onto the ties supporting them. I was a tightrope walker, practicing my craft while awaiting the circus train that would soon take me on to a new, exciting destination.

I learned fearlessness crossing the trestles—*my* trestles—first cupping an ear to the rail to listen for the approach of a locomotive and then stepping boldly onto the first bridge cross ties. Friends had warned me of reaching the "point of no return" halfway across a trestle only to hear the whistle of an approaching train. Too far to make it back, yet not close enough to make it on across, they told harrowing tales of having to shinny off the edge of the trestle and onto the bracing below. The trains passing through on *my* tracks and across *my* trestles were, of course, *my* trains. As they passed engineers always paid tribute to my sovereignty, blasting with their whistles as I mocked a pull on an imaginary whistle-cord. Now I was the engineer off to Chicago or New York or London or Australia. On another line I might be a wayfaring king of the road, just looking for blue skies and a hobo jungle.

I guess it was always better to *choose* not to be bored. This chapter is filled with ways other kids of the Good Old Days found to prove true the old adage: We were never bored.

—*Ken Tate*

© *Walking the Rails* by Jim Daly

Fun & Games Of Yesterday

By Flo N. Julien

When I was a child we did not mark the year by baseball, football and ice-hockey seasons. We divided it according to the games we played in the schoolyard.

When someone brought a skipping rope to school, we knew that skipping-rope season had begun. Before the week was out, all the little girls had brought their ropes, and after school, everyone skipped rope home again along the long, winding, leafy lanes.

Then, all at once, we knew that season had run out when a boy brought his top and whip. Days later, everyone had a top and whip, and was spinning bright tops for all they were worth at playtime. Red, blue, green and yellow tops spun like planets all over the schoolyard. There were, of course, always the experts who could keep theirs spinning long after everyone else's had toppled.

Then along came the season of hoops, signaled by the first boy or girl who came to school spinning a hoop. Soon we all had our big or little hoops, trying to keep them spinning alongside us as we ran along the lane until we reached home—a feat few of us managed.

Windy March brought kite season. Fathers fabricated marvelous paper kites for sons and daughters. Aloft they would soar, sometimes lost out of sight.

Windy March brought kite season. Fathers fabricated marvelous paper kites for sons and daughters. Aloft they would soar, sometimes lost out of sight. In a day when an airplane was seldom seen, kites were deemed very wonderful indeed. Parents and children alike shaded their eyes to gaze after them as they sailed over the trees, their strings sometimes tangling in the branches.

Fall brought the ancient game of conkers. These were chestnuts, which we hunted under the trees that lined the lanes we walked to school. The lovely, glossy brown nuts lay thickly everywhere after a windy autumn night. We selected the fattest ones for conkers.

Each of us tied a chestnut to a string, held it in the hand, and then dashed it against an opponent's conker until he lost his or we lost ours. The one who retained his or her conker unbroken won.

However, when I was very small, all the village parents got together and decided regretfully that we must put an end to the exciting game. That year, tragically, a small boy lost an eye when his opponent's conker flew up and hit him.

Less hazardous was the equally ancient game of hopscotch. In our old Lancashire town, the smooth flagstone pavement was ideal for chalking the squares needed for this hopping game. It consisted, I think, of throwing a pebble into a chalked square and then hopping into that square. It is more than 70 years since I played hopscotch, so perhaps my memory fails me as to the details. But I do remember doing a lot of hopping from square to square over our flagstoned sidewalks.

We had far fewer toys than children have nowadays, and they cost much less. But everyone had a Noah's ark. Poor families had a little one; the doctor's sons and daughters had a sumptuous one. But all were on the same model: bright red roof and grass-green walls. A set of farm animals and wild creatures came with the ark, and we could collect more because the village store sold wooden animals of all kinds for a few cents each.

Animals also were purchased eagerly for the small model farms many of us owned. The farmyard-and-farmhouse set was a very popular toy in 1925. We set up the house and the barn on the "farmland" provided—a wide swath of green with trim fences. We could buy optional "extras" such as a chicken coop, a pigsty, a duck pen or a sheep pen. The tiny metal painted animals that went with the farm were on sale everywhere for a few cents. How glad we were when we could earn a penny or two, doing chores round the home, so that we could run off to the village store to buy another cow, bull, duck or pony for our toy farm.

Many games had songs that went with them. Nuts in May was a song-and-dance game our great-grandparents had played. As we danced hand-in-hand around a girl, we sang the old tune:

Here we come gathering nuts in May,
Nuts in May,
Nuts in May.
Here we go gathering nuts in May,
On a cold and frosty morning.
Who shall we have to take her away,
Take her away,
Take her away?

Who shall we have to take her away
On a cold and frosty morning.

Skipping games had many old ditties handed down through the generations, too. One went:

Will I be married?
Yes or no!

A girl skipped until she tripped up on "yes" or "no." If she tripped on "yes," she would marry. Then the others asked:

Rich man, poor man,
Gentleman, thief?

She skipped to this rhyme; whichever she tripped on, she would marry. When it had been thus settled whom she would marry, everyone had to know what month she would wed in. So she now had to skip through the chanting of months till she tripped. Then we had to know what her wedding dress was made of, and again she would skip while we sang:

Silk, satin, cotton, wool …

And how would she get home from her wedding?

Horse-carriage, pony, bicycle, on foot …

Finally, when our bride was safely seen home, the next girl in the line had her turn. And so it went, down the line.

Games in those days were strictly divided by custom into those for boys and those for girls. Girls skipped rope; boys scorned it. Boys flew kites and played marbles more than girls did. Boys went to the brook and caught "minnies" (minnows) in jars for fishing bait. They went fishing with their dads while girls stayed home and played with their doll carriages, doll houses and doll cradles.

But no one ever thought they were being brainwashed into "stereotyped" roles. The word "brainwashing" came into use much later, as did the notion of some roles being stereotypes.

Girls didn't at all mind being given a pastry-cook set plus cap and apron and tiny stove, or a housemaid's set of broom and shovel for Christmas. Boys rejoiced in receiving a long box of tin soldiers in bright red uniforms with bayonets. They marshaled their armies on the living room floor and waged lively battles, with soldiers flying as the small boys chuckled. In those days, the thorny question of whether or not to let children play with war toys had not arisen. Fathers took for granted that boys enjoyed having a box of tin soldiers, just as they themselves and their grandpas had enjoyed years before.

Styles in toys never changed much. Year after year, the same toys appeared in the Christmas toyshops to the delight of each new generation.

There were heartaches and tears sometimes. The Christmas when I was 5, to my immense joy, I received a toy St. Bernard on wheels. It was big enough for me to sit on, a most gorgeous and adorable dog, and I took it to my heart at once and christened it "Bonzo." Two hours later, however, my cousins arrived to visit. Cousin Muriel, eight years old and quite plump, sat on Bonzo to take a ride around the room. During the third round, poor Bonzo's back capsized in the middle and he sank to the floor, an abject, sorrowful figure.

Distressed beyond belief, I screamed and wailed my grief, whereupon my uncle told me sternly that I was a crybaby and ordered me to stop that nonsense. No comfort was forthcoming; my parents were vexed, but that was all. Muriel's transgression was lightly glossed over and the incident was forgotten—by everyone but me.

At parties we played hunt the thimble, spin the plate, hide-and-seek and musical chairs. For hunting the thimble, one of the company would leave the room while the rest of us hid the thimble. Then he or she would be called back in and the company all began to sing softly: "How green you are, how green you are, how green … ," singing more loudly as the searcher approached the hiding place, more softly as he or she got farther away. When he finally found the thimble, he was rewarded with a crescendo of noise and cheers. Then another member of

Spinning a Hoop by Ron Delli Colli, House of White Birches nostalgia archives

the party left the room and again the thimble was hidden.

If there were many children, we played a rowdy game of blind man's bluff, while the sedate grown-ups played cards or dominoes. Various aunts and uncles always sang duets and solos 'round the piano in the front room while the rest of the party sipped cordials and juleps and relaxed.

We had memorable times when we were children more than 70 years ago, and they cost our elders very little. I wonder if today's youngsters will remember their complicated toys as long as I have remembered Bonzo, or have so much fun and laughter as we did when Aunt May found the thimble in the ribbon-and-net bird's nest in her hat! ❖

The Catfish Caper

By Rod C. Peabody

Back in 1926, when we moved to this whistle-stop town in Indiana, the first kid I met was Emmett. We were both about six years old and soon found that we liked to do the same things for fun.

After a couple of years we were real pals, running up and down the railroad tracks and out along the crick. We fished for goggle-eyes and chubs and had the time of our lives, swinging on grapevines like Tarzan, crawling across the creek on logs and trying to jump across the narrow places—sometimes successfully.

In the spring, half the town lined the riverbank, fishing for suckers. Of course, Emmett and I were right in the middle of that, too. That's where we heard about old Doc Lute's forbidden pond.

It was at the back end of his farm, close to the river. It was full of giant bluegills, bass and catfish—or so "they" said.

Well, Emmett and I just couldn't resist that, and later that summer, we made plans. We could sneak up on the river about a half-mile, take off our clothes and wade and swim across it, then fight our way through the eight-foot horseweeds for about 100 yards along the riverbottom and come out right at the pond. And that's just what we did.

The pond was in an old gravel pit with 25-foot banks about 100 yards across. In the middle of the horseweed patch was an old drainage ditch that we had to jump across. It was a slimy mess, well hidden by the weeds. The pond itself was lined with bushes; they were so thick that we had to hack through them to get our poles and lines into the water.

We had brought our short crick poles and plenty of worms and spare tackle. We were all set to catch those monsters in Doc Lute's pond. We weren't worried about old Doc; it was Charlie, the guy who did his farming, who scared us. He didn't like kids anywhere, particularly on the farm, near the pond.

We were pretty nervous, but we started fishing. All we caught were dinky little bluegills, three and four inches long. We fished about half an hour without catching anything big enough to take home.

Then Emmett started catching little catfish up close to the shore. And first thing you knew, we were trying to set the world's record for the smallest catfish.

Then a loud voice roared down from the top of the bank: "What are you kids doing down there?"

Well, Emmett grabbed his pole and tackle, I grabbed mine, and we took off, blasting through the horseweeds toward the river and safety! My pole got caught on a bush and I had to break the line to get it loose. By that time, Emmett was 20 feet ahead of me and going like a scared rabbit, popping those horseweeds like firecrackers. I was right behind him when suddenly, he plain disappeared.

I started to holler for him and then the ground dropped out from under *me*. In our terror, we'd forgotten about the four-foot drainage ditch that ran across the river bottom. Camouflaged by those tall horseweeds, we didn't see it and went *plunk! plunk!* right into it!

Emmett was trying to get his wind back and laugh at the same time, and so was I. We were rolling around in that sloppy mess of busted fishing poles, laughing like hyenas and trying to talk and get our wind and worry about Charlie. Finally Emmett gasped, "I don't care if Charlie does get me! I can't run another foot!" That brought another burst of laughs. Finally we were so weak that we just lay there and groaned.

Charlie didn't show up, and we finally collected our stuff and made it to the river. We waded across—clothes and all. We dumped the bluegills in the river and Emmett said, "That's the last time I listen to any wild rumors!"

"Yeah," I replied, "me too!"

Another lesson learned by Emmett and me. ❖

Lazy Day to Fish by Charles Berger, House of White Birches nostalgia archives

Dams, Forts & Tunnels

By Joseph L. Theis

I got to reminiscing the other day about what little boys do for fun and adventure today. I never see any of the boys in the neighborhood play in my old haunts—the woods, the railroad creek or the tunnel. These places were alive with laughter and shouts of children when I was a boy. Now they're quiet and forsaken. I think it's sad. We had imagination, and I think we had more fun.

My buddy, Bob Ransom, and I used to go down to the railroad creek. We'd spend hours chasing crawfish, and watching schools of minnows and the lightning speed of the water spiders. We made boats and sent them on perilous journeys with precious cargoes through pirate-infested waters.

Our greatest undertaking, however, was dam building. We worked all day, hauling stones and mud. Our tools were a couple of empty coffee cans, but to us they were mighty steam shovels. We weren't two boys playing; we were great engineers working to save humanity—the villages and towns below the dam—from the roaring waters.

Unfortunately, the railroad didn't share our point of view. We would return in a day or two and find our dam completely destroyed! Undaunted, we would rebuild it, wondering what act of fate had destroyed it—maybe secret agents, wanting to flood the make-believe villages? Maybe a bolt of lightning had caused a fissure, leading to its downfall. We knew, of course, that it was the railroad men, but we pretended otherwise.

This running battle with the railroad men lasted all summer. It seems the railroad didn't want four feet of water in their creek! The railroad men hid and tried to catch us, but we always knew they were there. A telltale trail of smoke from a cigarette, a cough or a hoarse whisper always alerted us to their presence. We pretended we didn't notice them and when they tried to sneak up on us, we jumped up and ran. We had secret kid-size paths and trails through the weeds and brush where no grown man could follow.

After we had eluded our pursers, we talked in excited whispers. They weren't railroad men; they were saboteurs, trying to wreak havoc on our villages and towns. We plotted new ways of combating them. We even took to sneaking out at night and rebuilding our dam by lantern light, heedless of the mosquitoes eating us alive. We persisted and we won our battle.

One afternoon we went down to the creek to check our dam. Much to our surprise, we found it intact, but with one addition. The railroad men had inserted a drain tile in the middle of our dam and lowered the water level to two feet. We decided to accept their peace offering and we were proud—proud because we had defeated the enemy and saved the towns.

The little pond that formed behind the dam was soon teeming with life. Crawfish, minnows, small fish and even frogs moved in and made it their home. Dragonflies were constantly buzzing over its surface. Monarch butterflies laid their eggs on the milkweed plants growing on its bank, and we watched in fascination as the eggs turned into little caterpillars. In no time at all they grew to three inches. We watched as they

> *The railroad didn't want four feet of water in their creek! The railroad men hid and tried to catch us, but we always knew they were there.*

spun their cocoons. We would keep a sharp eye on them in their pupal state. What a joy it was to watch the butterfly emerge, dry its glorious wings and, after gaining some strength, flutter its beautiful wings and fly off. We were proud of our pond. We thought we had accomplished a lot for a couple of eight-year-old boys!

We also had a little wooded area a couple of blocks from our house, and in the middle of it was a high hill. We built a log fort on top of that hill, dragging in old logs from all over the woods. Sometimes it took a whole day for us to get one oversized log up that hill. Ten determined boys can do wonders, however, and we pulled on ropes and pushed and rolled, and eventually it would end up in our fort.

It took three weeks of sweat and hard work to build that fort, but we were filled with self-esteem because we had built it by ourselves. It was ours to fight our enemies. Countless battles were fought on that hill.

There was a lonely pine tree on this hill, weathered and aged. It probably had been a sapling when the Sac and Fox Indians roamed the valley. It rose straight into the air, more than 100 feet tall. This was our lookout tree. We climbed to the top on its ladderlike branches. The whole valley could be seen from this lofty perch. The mighty Mississippi River, snaking its way downstream, was an awesome sight, breathtaking and beautiful.

We waited tensely below while someone climbed the tree. Would the enemy? Yes, they were coming! A wave of excitement passed through the fort as we began our feverish preparations. Cannons were pointed (short wooden logs), cannonballs were stacked (a pile of round stones), and muskets were loaded (homemade play rifles).

Someone spotted an enemy peeking around a sycamore tree and the battle began. We were hoarse from yelling all the "booms" and "bangs." During a lull in the battle, we drank lemonade and ate peanut-butter sandwiches from our meager supplies. Then the battle commenced again, and finally, down to our last musket ball, the enemy retreated. We had won again!

That old fort and the woods were a lot of fun, but they also taught us a lot. We learned to tell time and direction by the sun, and we learned that rattlesnakes don't attack unless they are bothered. We learned the habits of birds, rabbits and squirrels. We learned to snare rabbits, dressing and roasting them over a bed of coals. No one taught us these things; we learned by trial and error.

We also had potato roasts at night. We built a huge fire in the middle of our fort in a pit we had dug, then threw in potatoes, and while they roasted, we sang songs—*The Old Gray Mare*, *Pack Up Your Troubles in Your Old Kit Bag* and many others. When the fire was just a dull bed of coals, we fished out the potatoes, charred black but roasted clean through. We always burned our fingers cutting them open, but they were delicious.

When we had eaten our fill and the dark of night was upon us, one of the older boys told us a ghost story. Things got real quiet and we hung onto every word about goblins and witches that roamed in the night. An owl hooted and shivers went up our spines.

When the story was over, we put out the fire and started for home. It was scary walking through the woods at night. We cast fearful glances into the dark, lest some hobgoblin grab us and carry us off. When we reached the street, we boasted of our bravery and headed for home.

We had an initiation rite for those who wanted to join our gang. It was called "walking the tunnel." It was really a storm drain that started from a creek and ran three twisted blocks underground before draining into the railroad creek. My buddy Bob and I discovered the entrance one day and wondered if it was the same tunnel that drained into the railroad creek. There was only one way to find out, and after debating all the pros and cons, we decided to explore it. We went home and got a couple of candles and some farmer's matches and returned to the entrance.

One of the things that worried us most was water. At the entrance it was just a trickle a couple of inches deep, but at the railroad end— if that's where it did end—it would be more than two feet deep. And maybe it got deeper in the middle! Maybe we'd get halfway through and step in a big hole! Maybe we'd hit a gas pocket and the candle flame would ignite the gas and blow us up! There were a lot of "maybes" and we were both scared, but we knew we had to do it.

We finally decided that I'd go first. I'd tie a rope around my waist (I being the smaller one), and if I fell into a hole, Bob could pull me out. We went home, found some rope and returned to the tunnel entrance.

The tunnel was about five feet in diameter, and since we were only eight years old, we had plenty of headroom. We looked into the forbidding entrance, took a deep breath, and entered. After we had gone about 50 feet, the tunnel took a left turn. We lighted our candles and proceeded around the corner. We walked a bit further, stopped and looked back. We could see nothing of the tunnel entrance. Except for the light from our candles, we were in complete darkness. However, by now we knew we didn't have to worry about gas pockets, as a draft was blowing through the tunnel, almost extinguishing our candles.

I looked down at the water and froze in my tracks as a water moccasin swam leisurely through my legs. I turned and whispered to Bob, warning him. Bob looked down at the water as the snake stopped right in front of him. It lifted its head out of the water and its tongue flicked in and out. Then it lowered its head and swam between Bob's legs, toward the entrance. We both felt relieved after the snake had departed.

We walked a bit farther into the tunnel, brushing cobwebs out of our path. Bob gave a yell as a big black rat scurried past us and disappeared into a hole in the wall. Our hearts were beating like trip hammers. What if we ran into a pack of them? We'd be eaten alive! Our vivid imaginations added to our fears. We talked things over a bit and decided to continue.

We walked around another corner and I screamed and dropped my candle. Huge centipedes, about five inches long, were running all over the tunnel, fleeing the light into cracks in the walls. We had seen plenty of centipedes before, but none this large. I recovered my candle and relit it with shaking hands.

The water was now about a foot deep, and

from the glow of our candles, we could see that it was getting higher on the tunnel walls. We proceeded farther and soon the water was over our knees. I picked my steps warily, lest I step into a deep hole.

We had almost decided to go back when we saw another turn in the tunnel. And like all true explorers, we had to see what was around the next bend. We were glad we did, because there was daylight and the tunnel's end, less than 70 feet away. The water was up to our hips, but we joyously splashed though it.

We sat down on the creek bank outside the tunnel in the warm sunshine to rehash our adventure. I'll tell you, we were two happy kids! It was then that we decided that every member of our gang had to go through the tunnel alone, with just a candle.

When a new boy moved into the neighborhood and wanted to join our gang, we told him about the tunnel and set a date for his initiation, usually in about a week. When one little kid named Davey asked me about the tunnel, I told him there was nothing to be disturbed about, and that he shouldn't worry when the water got up to his neck. Then I added, "Of course, you're about six inches shorter than me, but don't let it bother you. You'll probably make it." I walked off, leaving the poor kid standing there with his mouth open.

After about a week of this, a kid could get pretty rattled. He heard about the snakes, rats, huge centipedes and deep holes. Surprisingly, however, not one kid ever refused to walk the tunnel. He entered it trying to hide his doubts and fears, but when he came out the other end, he was a different kid. He was a proud kid.

I find these childhood adventures a great help in my adult world. Whenever I get discouraged about some endeavor, I think back to that dam and how persistence won, and I take heart. Whenever a problem seems impossible, I remember how a bunch of eight- and nine-year-old boys did the impossible, getting a huge log, 25 feet long and a foot and a half in diameter, up a steep hill, and I put forth new effort. When life gets dark and full of fear, I think of the tunnel and I go on, for I know there's a light at the end. ❖

Barefoot Games

By Bethene A. Larson

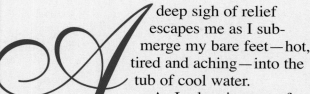deep sigh of relief escapes me as I submerge my bare feet—hot, tired and aching—into the tub of cool water.

As I relax, images of ghost children from 50 years ago flit across my memory, and I smile as I recall how good the cool water felt when my cousins and I ran barefoot on the scorching Kansas earth.

"Let's run the lane!" one of us would shout as the sun made its way across the summer sky, baking the clay surface of the country lane into a hot, dusty crust.

Squealing with the exuberance of youth, ever ready to accept a challenge, each of us would grab an empty 2-pound coffee can from under the back porch and rush to the cattle-watering tank.

The object of the game was to fill the old coffee can with water from the tank, then run barefoot to the end of the half-mile lane. When we reached the crossroads where the mailbox was nailed to the post, we would make a speedy retreat back to the water tank.

Sounds simple, but the challenge was to make the can of water last to the end of the journey. When our feet became too hot to run another step, we stopped, poured some water onto our feet, enjoyed a few moments of relief, then continued until it was necessary to stop again.

The winner was the person who returned to the water tank first, but the only prize was the satisfaction of surviving the "agony" and the success of rationing the precious water. There was also that childish pride of being first to yell, "I win!"

The winner was the person who returned to the water tank first, but the only prize was the satisfaction of surviving the "agony" and the success of rationing the precious water.

When all six of us were back at the water tank, we sat on the water-soaked, moss-covered old board balanced across one end of the tank. As we dangled our suntanned legs in the cool water, we laughed over our adventurous journey of self-torture. Overhead the windmill squeaked, mocking our foolishness.

One memorable day as we gleefully ran our familiar route, a long rattlesnake crawled out of the ditch and slithered across the lane. My cousin, Elda, a few feet ahead of me, screamed a warning to those of us who followed, and we lost no time in retracing our steps, not stopping once to pour soothing water on our scorching feet. When we reached the house, we all shouted at once, which brought a quick response from the adults within.

Uncle Carl bravely killed the huge snake. Then he warned us about playing our barefoot game, explaining that if there was one snake, there was a good chance others were nesting nearby.

It was hard to submit to the restrictions. But our regrets were short-lived, for we soon became involved in cleaning out the corn crib where we had plans to set up a clubhouse, play school or entertain ourselves with the barn kittens. Only the mice that occasionally observed our activities interfered with our pleasure there.

I don't recall that we ever asked, "What's there to do?" Our imaginations knew no boundaries, and the challenges were never exhausted. The farm held too many treasures yet untouched, adventures undiscovered, and summertime was too precious to waste. ❖

There Was Fun Before Now

By Ruth Corbett

Our children and grandchildren seem to think that we had little, if any, amusement or entertainment in our "archaic" times way back in the 1930s. But all of us from that era recall many diversions. You may not have indulged in all of them, but some will bring misty-eyed smiles.

Much of our social life took place in our homes. I remember rolling up the Axminster rug, putting a foxtrot record on the Victrola—maybe by the Paul Whiteman Band—and dancing. It was luxurious when the advent of radio brought continuous music without the need for cranking the phonograph and turning the records over.

Did you do the Castle Walk, Black Bottom, Charleston, Suzie Q, Truckin', Varsity Drag, Lambeth Walk or Big Apple? Maybe your taste ran to Latin rhythms such as the Continental, Congeroo, Rumba or Conga.

Card parties were prevalent, but if we played bridge, it was the popular "auction bridge," not the "contract" variety. Euchre, casino, pinochle, rummy and hearts all had devotees—and hasn't poker always been around?

We might trip over a wicket in the yard because we played croquet often enough that we left the equipment in place for the next game. Some men we knew donned "plus fours" to enjoy a round of golf; they called their clubs "sticks." My nonplaying father disdainfully called golf "hitting the pill"—a silly pastime in his eyes, even though John D. Rockefeller had been photographed taking a whack at the "pill" when he was in his 90s.

We also flocked to the movie palaces for diversion. Whether we enjoyed melodramas, musical extravaganzas, gangster stories or screaming at ghostly hands reaching out of walls, there was something for every taste—and there was *always* Laurel and Hardy!

The live stage offered some of the all-time giants of acting. If we couldn't get to the Great White Way, we might still see them in traveling companies. One stock company stayed in our town for months at a time, offering a new play each week.

We made some of our music for our own amusement. Did anyone not have at least one would-be musician in the family? Popularity was assured for those who could passably "tickle the ivories," play the "squeeze box" or any other instrument. Singing to the plinking of a ukulele was fun; the tune might be *The Sweetheart of Sigma Chi*.

If we were not dancing on the living room floor, we might be visiting one of the city ballrooms, some of which had summer outdoor "gardens." I was always fascinated by the globe made of little pieces of mirror, which hung in the center of the room revolving slowly, reflecting changing colored lights. And dancing in a ballroom was always exciting if we were with that best girl or beau!

No, we were not one whit less amused, diverted or entertained than those who today enjoy gyrating to the beat of whatever the current craze is. We didn't slouch in front of the "boob tube"; instead, we slouched in the seats of the Bijou, the Orpheum or whatever the local theater was called, to emote along with Clara Bow or that heart-twisting matinee idol, John Gilbert.

And besides all of that, how could I forget the taffy pulls, quilting bees, and gaping at a "human fly" or crazy flagpole sitter? Who says we didn't have fun way back then? ❖

My Brother & Me

By William J. Webbe

When you were a kid, did you ever play imaginary games with your older brother? If you have, you know how frustrating it can be.

Imagination back in the 1930s accounted for 50 percent of the games we played; memory was 25 percent, and the remaining 25 percent was the ingenuity we needed to make whatever equipment we needed.

There were four children in the Webbe family. I was the last, so I was destined to be the baby of the family forever. This can be a blessing, except when you're playing games with an older brother who will always dominates the game.

My brother, Frank, was three years older than I was. It wasn't that he was a bully or tyrant; it was just that the direction of the game was his by birthright, and if I infringed, he let me know about it in no uncertain terms.

It didn't matter what game we played—I was the bad guy. I can't remember ever playing with Frank when I was the good guy. I came close once; we were on the same side, but before the game was half over, I was suddenly switched to the villain. I guess it made the game a little more interesting.

Of course, being the villain, I had to die. It didn't matter how—I could be shot with a gun or arrow, strangled, hung, thrown off a building, cliff, or out of an aircraft, or poisoned. Whatever the means, you can be sure that I was to die. Sometimes I died two or three times in the same game. And I performed the best death scenes; I should have received the Academy Award. Cagney and Bogart had nothing on me.

I never seemed to suffer a minor wound in our games; it was always fatal. But if Frank allowed himself to be shot by me, it was always superficial. He never had to worry about dying.

This brings to mind a game of cops and robbers that Frank and I were playing one day in the backyard. As usual, I was the bad guy, B.O. Plenty or Dillinger. In this game, I escaped from Frank by hiding behind a tree behind the garage. The tree was in a great position; from it I could see in both directions.

I waited for what seemed an eternity for Frank to come after me. I couldn't understand what was keeping him, and I was getting very jittery. For some reason, I looked up at the garage roof. There was my sneaky brother, cautiously inching his way back to the edge of the garage. He didn't know I was watching him. I had him this time for sure. There was no escape. I could have shot him right there, but I waited.

Frank peeked over the edge, thinking I would be directly under him. I couldn't believe my good fortune when he slid off the roof right in front of my hiding place. As he peeked around the corner of the garage to see if I was there, I pointed my 50-shot Dick Tracy cap pistol at his back. I was almost touching him; I fired as fast as I could. (Back shooting was legal in our games.)

Now, if you have played cops and robbers with an older brother, you will understand what happened next. If not, you won't believe it. My brother, Frank, being as fair as the day is long, fell to the ground, rolled over once or twice, yelled "MISSED," fired his gun pointing somewhere up in the tree and yelled the magic word that only works for older brothers: "GOTCHA!"

At this point, a younger brother had two choices: fall down, play dead and live; or tell his older brother he was wrong, that *he* was dead, and then try to outrun him to the safety of the house and Mom. Being three years younger and smaller, and not being too swift of foot, I chose to play dead. It was less painful. I could never win.

Sometimes I liked to play by myself. In these games I was always a winner. My imagination changed ordinary household objects right before my eyes. A bed footboard became my trusted steed, carrying me across the field of battle at the head of a great army. Then, in the blink of an eye, it became a large elephant as I rode alongside Tarzan into a great adventure. My peaceful bed pillows might become my dreaded enemy and the edge of my bed a cliff that reached down to a watery grave.

The game I liked to play most by myself was Westerns. Perhaps it was because I knew this time period best. There were more Western movies than anything else; at least it seemed that way. The games we played were mostly made up from movies we saw.

Westerns featured the likes of Roy Rogers, Gene Autry, Hopalong Cassidy, Wild Bill Elliot, Cisco Kid, Wild Bill Hickok, Bat Masterson and Wyatt Earp, to name a few. On the other side of the coin we had Jesse James and his brother, Frank (no relation to my brother Frank, although I sometimes wondered), the Dalton brothers, Billy the Kid, Johnny Ringo and the Sundance Kid. We had them all, good and bad. It was difficult to choose. I could be anyone that I wanted. After all, I was the director when I played alone.

Another reason I liked to play Westerns was that I had more equipment for the game. I had a beautiful silver scrolled six-shooter with a disc instead of a roll of caps, and after it was fired six times, it had to be reloaded. It truly *was* a six-shooter. The six-shooter had a "real ivory" plastic handle with a long-horned steer's head on both sides, and it fit snugly into a brown holster that had silver and ruby stud inlays and six silver bullets on the belt. Wearing that gun, I was Jesse James and Wyatt Earp all rolled up into one.

I could play for hours in my room all by myself, imagining one episode after another— from good guy to bad guy and even somewhere in between. Imagination was all that I needed, and without Frank around to "direct" me, I had imagination to spare. Yup, I could fight off a murderous band of marauding savages, sustaining only two or three minor arrow wounds. Even wounded as I was, I could still defeat the deadly bed pillows single-handed.

Frank and I were both in the Army—finally on the same side, although not at the same time. Frank was in World War II and I was in Korea. Both of us returned home safe and sound.

When I was 26 years old, married and with two children, I went on the Port Washington Police Force. Frank married a year after I did and also joined a police force, becoming one of New York City's finest. We were again on the same side, now at the same time, and still in the game of cops and robbers. Except now, both of us were good guys.

We lived and worked about 40 miles apart but still found time to see each other. We shared many Sunday dinners down at Mom's house. It made Mom happy to see her two boys getting along so well.

Frank often called me to play golf; he was fanatical about the game. We played as long as there was no snow on the ground. One year we played in January.

During hunting season we went to the Adirondack Mountains for a week. Before the Northway was built, it took us about eight hours to get to our hunting spot, North Creek, in upstate New York. The Adirondacks are so vast that Frank and I never saw a live deer in the woods, let alone got one. In the three years we hunted there, the only living things we saw were a chipmunk and a man walking through the woods on his way to church in his Sunday best.

My wife, Helen, and I decided to move upstate to the Catskills after our daughter, Deborah, and our son, Billy, went out in the world on their own. Frank and I still play golf in the summer. It's fun just being together.

We sometimes joke about the things we did when we were kids, and reminisce about the good times we had in our childhood. But to this day, Frank still refuses to admit that I really got him that time behind the garage, back in the Good Old Days. ❖

The Great Crate Race

By George Lamb

In 1924, three very important events took place in the United States. Calvin Coolidge was elected president, I celebrated my 10th birthday, and the Great Orange-Crate Race took place in my hometown.

To tell the tale, first of all, I need to explain something. Whenever I think of that race in the late summer of 1924, I always think of it as a very major event. Hence, I think of it in capital letters, and I shall refer to it here in like manner.

Of course, I had nothing to do with the first national event, and the second came as many others have since on an annual basis. But the third, the Great Orange-Crate Race, not only remains a clear and prominent part of my memory, but is one event in which I most certainly had a hand in determining the outcome.

Remember the orange crate? It had two equal sections of thin wood with strong wooden end pieces and a solid center of slab wood dividing it into equal parts. Flimsy paper labels on each end proclaimed the origin of the oranges.

The thought of building orange-crate racers came to Bobby Henderson, Billy Witt and me one afternoon while we were on our way home from the Family Theatre. We had seen the matinee of *Monsieur Beaucaire*, featuring Rudolph Valentino and Bebe Daniels.

Walking home, we carried out an imaginary sword duel like the one we had seen in the

My racer was heavier to begin with, and I made it heavier by attaching two inverted tin cans on the front for headlights, two empty tuna fish cans painted red on the back for taillights, and a great big gallon bean can on the top to simulate a searchlight.

movie. Billy almost dueled me right over the side of the bridge when we light-footed it across the Rock River. He was always lighter on his feet than I was. Being much fatter than the other two, I constantly lost in events like fencing duels, gunfights, footraces and the like.

As we passed the F.C. Sproul Northside Cash Grocery, we stopped to look at the Saturday afternoon papers. Bobby wanted to see what would be on at the show the rest of the week, while Billy enjoyed the sports page. I wanted to see the comics, especially those about *Washington Tubbs* and *Freckles and His Friends*.

As we were standing there on the sidewalk looking at Mr. Sproul's papers, one of the older guys who worked there on Saturdays came out to talk to us. Among other things, he said that he had just thrown out several orange crates, and if we wanted them, we should pick them up before Mr. Spotts came along with his wagon to haul them away.

The other two boys and I had been looking for new crates for some time, so we went around back. Each of us took two of the better orange boxes stacked near the alley.

We decided that we would store them in my garage because it was the biggest. Also, my dad had a pretty good workshop at the rear of the building and we would need to use many tools for our project. We were going to build an orange-crate racer, the kind that was so popular then.

By the time we made it to my house, I was

First Prize at the Crate Race by Charles Berger, House of White Birches nostalgia archives

almost beat. The other two didn't seem to mind carrying those crates, though; in fact, for almost a block, Bob had balanced one on his head and carried the other in his arms. I lugged mine along, dragging the ends on the ground.

Arriving home in such a worn-out condition, we decided just to store the crates and work on them during the next week. Each of us was to secure his own extra equipment: tin cans, skates, poles, beams, and other things like that.

Bright and early Monday morning, Bob and Bill showed up at our house. By the time I had dressed and eaten breakfast, both of them had already begun to construct their orange-crate racers. My sister, Donna, was sitting on a ledge, watching them and making her usual observations about the way things were being done. No one paid her much mind.

Bob had attached his crate to a 4-foot 2-by-4 he had brought with him, hammering several large nails to connect them. Billy's was not as complete, as he was just starting to attach the old skates he had brought from home to the bottom of the pushbeam he would later attach to the orange crate.

By noon, all three of us were pretty well along with our own orange-crate racers. I had a skate at each end of the two boards I had to use, meaning that both my skates and an extra pair were being utilized. (My racer had to be made doubly strong to accommodate my extra weight, you know.)

Both Bob and Bill had made their racers as light as possible for better downhill speed. They had attached half-skates at each end of a center beam, and nailed a broom handle with the broom end sawed off to the top of the crate for handles. They had attached the crate itself on the front of the main beam using as few nails as possible.

That afternoon, all three of us added the necessary accessories to our racers. Bob's just had one tin can nailed to the center of the crate for a simulated light. He also used red paint to paint "Henderson's Flash Racer" on the front.

Billy put a 1921 license plate from his dad's old Ford Tudor sedan on the front of his racer. He also painted the entire creation bright blue, and then added white lettering—"Witt's Blue Streak"—diagonally across the front panel.

My racer was heavier to begin with, and I made it heavier by attaching two inverted tin cans on the front for headlights, two empty tuna fish cans painted red on the back for taillights, and a great big gallon bean can on the top to simulate a searchlight. Also, I put handle grips from my bike on the ends of the round pole I used for handles, and put a signboard across the front.

The signboard was about eight inches wider than the front of my orange crate racer, a fact that would later cause me great discomfort. The lettering—done by Donna the night before with a slight female scrawl to it—read, "The World's Greatest Racer." (I guess I figured that if you thought so, you should tell everyone else.)

Each of us took turns testing the others' racers. We pushed off along our driveway, out onto the sidewalk. A slight decline in front of the Nelsons' house next-door gave us a taste of real speed.

About 5 o'clock or so, Mom sent Donna out with a message that dinner would be ready soon, and that we had better clean up our mess. Rather than taking their racers home, the guys left them in our yard. We had decided to try running them over a distance, and we agreed to reconvene later that evening.

After supper, I showed Dad the three racers. He said each one was very nice and displayed good, solid workmanship; he never once asked why mine was so much heavier looking and bulkier than the other two. Donna did, though. At least my dad was polite!

We had a great time that night taking our racers all over the neighborhood. Of course, I tagged along a poor third, huffing and steaming to keep my contraption up with the other two lightweights.

For several days and nights thereafter, the three of us contented ourselves with working on the crate racers, repairing minor damage, adding and subtracting from them when the whim hit, and generally enjoying ourselves a great deal.

Toward the end of the week, Donna came running to tell us that some other kids were heading up the street, pushing orange-crate racers like ours. She was all out of breath and it took her a piece of time to get the facts out. By the time she finished telling us that the guys coming were the Hanson, Hughes and Sinow guys from the South Side, they were in our driveway. Each had an orange-crate racer a lot like ours in most respects.

First off, these four guys (one Hanson, one Hughes, and the Sinow twins, David and Jackie) were always giving us a hard time. They had grown up together, just as Bobby, Billy and I had. It's not that we really disliked each other; we just were always competing with them.

As we stood around comparing racers, someone suggested that we all go for a ride around the neighborhood. We ended up at the top of the Brinton Avenue hill, and there we talked about going down that steep, two-block hill that ended in a wide grassy area next to the riverbank.

We had never gone down that hill before. Not only was it steep and dangerous, but if you didn't stop just right, you could catapult right along that grass into the river.

The others had almost decided to take a chance and all go down together. In fact, "Deacon" Hanson and Billy Witt were lining up their racers to start. I had to think up some excuse so that I would not have to travel down that hill.

"Wait a minute, you guys!" I gasped. "You don't want to go down that dumb hill for nothing! *Anybody* can do that!"

They all turned and looked at me, thinking I was out of my skull or something. After a few more quick, deep breaths, I calmed down enough to tell them about the sudden idea I had just had.

"Why not have a race down the hill, all starting together, and we can see who has the fastest and best racer?" I asked somewhat lamely.

But the idea must have been a good one, because before you could say "Gloria Swanson," all of us had lined up our racers at the top of the street, ready to push off. Donna had joined the group by now and was appointed official starter, with Mr. Post, the mailman, pressed into service to determine the winner.

As Mr. Post had to be at the finish line, the race was slightly delayed while he made his mail stops on both sides of the street down the two-block hill. He must have mentioned the Great Orange-Crate Race to his patrons because heads popped out of doors and windows along the route until we had acquired a rather respectable audience.

Then Mr. Kelchner, the police chief, drove up in the city's Dodge Brothers four-passenger coupe that was considered the police squad car. He stopped and got out to ask us what we

Mr. Kelchner, the police chief, drove up in the city's Dodge Brothers four-passenger coupe that was considered the police squad car. He stopped and got out to ask us what we were up to.

were up to. Our plan to race down the hill must have met with his approval because he just smiled and told us to be careful. The next thing we knew, he had driven around the block and was parked down at the end of the route, waiting for Mr. Post.

So there we were, seven guys and their homemade orange-crate racers at the top of a very steep hill, with a starter, a mailman and a police officer as judges of the winners of everything.

The people who lived along the route were ready to see the action. Even the new family, the Ostergrants, were arranged along their front porch steps. The kids, Jana, Matt, Lee, Andy and little baby Billy, were all there with their mother, who sewed as she watched us.

Pretty soon Mr. Post waved his arms to signal that he and Chief Kelchner were ready. Thriving in the attention of so many people, Donna stepped up to the curb and waited for complete quiet. In fact, she waited so long to say, "Get ready, get set, go!" that Billy Witt yelled at her to get it over with before it was time for him to go home. Donna glared at him for cutting her time in the spotlight, then dropped her arm and screamed "Go!" at the top of her lungs.

We had expected a bit more notice, so only Deacon and Bob got started right away. Right behind them went Del Hughes, Billy's "Blue Streak," and the twins' racers. You know who was last getting started, don't you? Me, of course, as I had slipped to my knees when I tried to push off. I recovered quickly, though, and was gone in a slow flash.

Deacon and Bob were a bit ahead of the pack at the halfway point over the first cross street. They were really moving. Then Billy swerved when he reached the cross street, causing him to pull to his right. He hit Jackie's racer, which in turn smacked into David's, and both of them landed in a heap.

Little Del Hughes was only a bit behind them, and he had to turn very sharply to avoid the pileup. He made it around them alright, but he couldn't straighten out in time to avoid the curb, and as his racer bounced up over it, he flew off. Del landed, unhurt but with pride ruffled, on Mr. Trickel's lawn. But his racer continued until it had ripped out a section of the Trickels' rose hedge and crashed head-on into their porch.

From my vantage point in the rear, I had seen all this take place as I approached the halfway point. In that same split-second, I also looked down the hill and saw Bobby and Deacon heading their racers into each other in a misguided attempt to keep the other from crossing the winner's line first. All they managed to accomplish was cause a two-racer crack-up about midway down the second block of the course. Bobby and Deacon fell in opposite directions as their racers collided with a loud *smack*. Both jumped right up and started throwing punches at each other and screaming like two demented banshees.

As I said, I saw all this action in front of me as I came down the hill. To tell the truth, I had pushed my racer only a few feet at the very beginning and thereafter allowed it to gain speed on its own, without further help from me. I was simply holding on for dear life as it went faster and faster—but at least it went in a straight direction, being heavier and more solid than the other speedsters.

I steered around the first jumble of Billy and the twins. When I passed, they were all arguing about whose fault the wreck had been. My racer skimmed the cross street with a bounce that made my eyes bug, and I barely cleared the big fight going on between Deacon and Bobby. Off to my left, I could see little Del Hughes being bawled out by Mr. Trickel over the condition of his rose hedge.

My racer proceeded down the hill. I could see Mr. Post swinging his mailbag back and forth like a flag, just like the end of the big car races. He was excited about seeing the race from his vantagepoint and had walked up the course a few steps.

As my racer neared him, he began to shout that I was the winner. He swung his bag, thinking he had a winner's flag. But just as I passed him on the way to victory, that great big heavy leather mail pouch hit the signboard that stuck out from the front of "The World's Greatest Racer." The force of the bag's impact knocked my racer off-balance and me with it. The racer tipped over and stopped immediately, as I fell in a clump on the street. By then, Donna was standing over my inert frame, hollering at me to get up.

"You ain't won yet! You ain't over the line yet. Get up, get up! You ain't won yet!" she kept screaming over and over.

But I didn't really care. I was so surprised to hear my dignified sister use the undignified word "ain't" that I didn't hear the rest of what she was saying. Also, my body was beginning to feel the effects of the crash.

It must have been a rare sight indeed, though, looking up that street that day in 1924. Neighbors were all running out to help the racers, Mr. Trickel was still yelling at Del, and the whole Ostergrant clan was jumping up and down.

Deacon and Bobby were being separated by Chief Kelchner, who could hardly keep a hold on them, he was laughing so hard. The twins had decided that the other was the cause of their crack-up, so they were arguing loudly, too. Bill Witt was just standing in the middle of the pile of broken orange crates, looking rather sad.

And me—there I was, farther along the race route than any of them, but still not a winner—at least, I hadn't been declared as such by anyone of official status. As soon as Mr. Post hit my racer, he left to complete his route. I guess he didn't want to involve the U.S. Postal Service in such a fracas.

So no one ever did win the Great Orange-Crate Race—and I never, *ever* have gotten my sister Donna to admit that she used the word "ain't." ❖

Privileged Kids of Yesteryear

By Ida May Both

I wonder if our children are as privileged as we like to think they are. Living in a rather poor neighborhood during most of my childhood in the Depression, I had many joys that were never known by my children.

Take the joy of picking berries. At the edge of our road were fields where patches of wild berries grew, unclaimed by anyone in particular. Berry season drew all the kids from a mile around. Since there were more kids than the berries could satisfy, the trick was to rise earlier than the others and pick the berries that had ripened overnight, carefully looking underneath for luscious clusters that might have been missed by more careless pickers. Oh, what joy to carry home a pail full, enough for the family's breakfast! We braved thorns and mosquitoes—even snakes—and we had wounds to show for it, but it was fun.

Our neighborhood also boasted an abandoned orchard, including several worm-eaten cherry trees and an apple tree. We played in the orchard all the time, and we gobbled up the cherries when the first flush of pink appeared on their skins. We gave the birds so much competition that they even went elsewhere for worms. The apples were always eaten green, too, and our mothers credited them for all our tummy aches. But it was exciting.

One big cherry tree stood like the grand prize; it grew on a neighbor's lawn, just across the street from us. (We were considered lucky to live so close to it.) Of course, the neighbors had priority; those cherries were theirs, and no respectable child went into their yard to pick from that tree.

Yet there were rains and windstorms that brought little showers of cherries and shouts of delight, for any cherries found on the lawn and sidewalk were generally conceded to belong to any child who found them. These luscious, black, sweet cherries were such a prize that two or three was a high score for any storm, even when you lived right across the street.

Then there was the old swimming hole—only waist-deep and complete with water spiders, bloodsuckers and mud, but the best-loved spot in town. It was close, it was free, and we all went there. Many didn't have swimsuits, so the little ones wore only their panties and the older girls wore old dresses. There were no bathing beauties here and no one cared.

Fall meant nut hunting and other pleasures. Nuts weren't too plentiful around our neighborhood, but if you got in on the secrets, you learned where to find butternuts and black walnuts within walking distance (and anyplace within 10 miles was walking distance for us).

We spent hours and hours spreading out the walnuts to dry and then hulling and cracking them—first the soft outer shell, then the stone-hard inner shell—before finally digging the meat out of the crevices. We had walnut-stained fingers for weeks afterward, but it was all part of the deal.

Sliding down a hill on cardboard is every bit as much fun as a sled ride. Sometimes the city blocked off a hilly road or two for the kids' use.

We picked flowers in the spring and explored all year-round. We were ingenious in many ways. We made play furniture from cockleburs and arrows from dried weeds.

Now kids sit in the middle of a room with expensive toys and say, "There's nothing to do!" I think they've missed out on the privileges—poor kids! ❖

Sledding on Dead Man's Run

By Mary Sue Utley

The sounds of laughter pealed through the air. Glancing through the window, I saw two young neighbor boys sliding down our snow-covered driveway on their plastic sleds, whooping and hollering as they glided the short distance. I smiled as I remembered my own sledding days years ago, back in the early 1950s.

Across from my childhood home in Salt Lake City, Utah, a cluster of hills lay in the distance. One winter, a succession of snowstorms left a deep blanket of snow, providing some excellent sledding. Then, on Christmas morning, I found a new wooden sled under the tree. (Actually, it was a used one, but I didn't mind.)

Along with my brother, sister and a handful of neighbor kids, I pulled my sled down the street about the distance of two city blocks, then headed south through an open field, up toward the most treacherous spot on the hill—Dead Man's Run. My excitement mixed with fear as I tramped through the crusty snowdrifts.

Dead Man's Run, as it had been dubbed by the other kids, was a path leading straight down about 100 feet—at least it *seemed* that way—to a tangled mass of bushes. At that point, the trail veered off to the right and around a bend butting up against another hill. If you didn't steer sharply at the right moment, you would plummet into the middle of those awful bushes.

And they were not like the puny sagebrush, which were plentiful on the hills. No, these bushes were huge and filled with thorns, the kind that loved to chew up sleds. As we edged past the curve, I grimaced when I caught sight of smooth, long runner tracks leading into those ominous bushes. *Would that be my fate?* I wondered. I heaved a sigh and continued up the hill.

No, I thought. *Today is my day! Today I'll be victorious!* My heart pounding, I trudged forward. My laborious breathing turned to steam in the frigid air and the cold bit at my throat. After reaching the summit, I held back, not wanting to be the first to descend.

Without a moment's hesitation, my brother Jim threw his body onto his sled with full force. He made it look easy. He yelled like a conquering warrior as he zoomed down the hill.

My older sister was next. Her high-pitched scream held more panic, but she too made it safely to the bottom. The others took their turns one at a time. Looking down into the large ravine, I stood frozen with fear. I gladly allowed everyone to go ahead of me.

I was still standing in the same spot when everyone made it to the top again. *This is it,* I thought. *No more stalling*! I took a deep breath, mustering up all the courage I could. With adrenaline pumping, I slowly stretched out over my sled and gripped the handles.

Jim secured my sled as I positioned myself. I lacked the courage to start like he did—pushing back and forth, and throwing his full weight down on the sled. I had tried it before, and always landed off-center.

I timidly called out, "One, two … two and a half …" Jim groaned. "Wait, Jimmy, wait! I'm not ready," I muttered.

"Would you just go!" he barked.

"OK, OK," I said. "One, two, three—go!" I cried meekly.

"Geronimo!" yelped Jim, as he pushed the sled off with my body clinging for dear life.

A half-second later I changed my mind, but it was too late. I careened down the hill at a record-breaking speed. Voices behind me were yelling, "Look out! Look out, Sue!" The cold powder blew harshly in my face as I closed my eyes and gritted my teeth.

It's a wonder I wasn't battered and bruised by the wild bumping as the sled flew over the moguls. I managed to squint open one eye, trying to keep a sharp lookout for the bush waiting for me below, like a hunter with his snare.

Panic engulfed me as the yards turned to feet. Suddenly, the bush loomed in front of me, mere inches away. My hands froze on the handles; I couldn't steer. Paralyzed with fear, there

was nothing I could do except lower my head and get ready for impact. *Whooze! Crunch!* Twisted limbs went flying everywhere; fortunately, they were the bush's, not mine.

The crash knocked the wind out of me. I lay very still on the icy ground, staring at the gray sky above, while my brother and sister ran down the hill to see if I was still alive. As soon as I caught my breath, they told me everything I had done wrong.

I finally made the perilous turn successfully once or twice a few years later, but not without receiving several scratches from the bushes blocking the path. They were my badges of courage in days when sledding hills seemed steeper, longer and teeming with danger.

More squeals of laughter pierced the night, drawing me back to the present. I smiled knowingly as I watched the two youngsters heading home, dragging their sleds. I'm sure they had a good time, but my driveway is no match for Dead Man's Run. ❖

Uphill Sledding by Alan Foster © 1931 SEPS: Licensed by Curtis Publishing

JOHN FALTER

Snow Days—A Gift

By Sandra Scott

When I was young, the best winter surprise did not occur on Christmas morning. Oh, I loved Christmas, but I knew when it was approaching. I counted the days in eager anticipation of Christmas morning when I could open all the wonderful things Santa had brought. The best surprise was the one I didn't plan on ... the one that was just waiting for me when I woke up in the morning ... a snow day off from school.

Nothing made me jump out of bed faster than the words my mother yelled up the stairs: "School's closed!" I would bounce out of bed and rush to the window to see the wonderland that had been created during the night. I would huff on the window to melt the thin layer of ice and scratch away the lacy frost, eager to see just how much snow had fallen while I was asleep. The trees were weighted down with a thick layer of snow, clumps dropping off at the slightest stirring. There was a heavy quietness to the morning as the cold blanket of snow wrapped the world in warmth and security.

With great care and precision I would move my arms up and down and my legs from side to side. Then came the hard part: getting up without making a deep "sit" spot.

Determined to enjoy every minute of my gift, I would dress in my warmest clothes and, drawn by the aroma of sizzling bacon, rush downstairs. My mind was racing, trying to decide what to do first. The snow brought a wonderful assortment of new things to do.

After gulping down breakfast, I dressed for the occasion. Gone forever are the bulky wool snowsuits that collected the snow in miniature snowballs and the metal-clasp boots that required many socks; at least one pair went on over the shoes to keep my feet warm and dry.

A multicolored handmade hat, muffler and mittens completed my outfit. It took two people to put on the finishing touches. Mother knew just how to fix the mittens and cuffs so that no snow would get in.

Stepping outside—and looking like the Pillsbury doughboy—I was ready. The brightness of the sun made me squint and the cold hit my lungs like a sharp knife. Snow diamonds sparkled in the crisp air.

The world had no sharp edges; the snow had sculpted everything into gentle curves and swirls. Rooflines were softened by a thick layer of white fluff that curled down over the edges. Mother Nature had put her own special frosting on the world.

After a few seconds I was acclimatized. My eyes now searched the unbroken mantle of white for the perfect spot—one that wouldn't be in the way of later plans, one that would give the best viewing.

When I found the best spot, I would take a giant step backward into the snow, and as lightly as I could, I would flop backward into the fluffy, white snow. With great care and precision I would move my arms up and down and my legs from side to side. Then came the hard part: getting up without making a deep "sit" spot. Stepping out, I would turn to admire my perfect snow angel—someone to watch me while I played.

Next I would check the garage roof to see if the snow had drifted high enough so that I could climb up one side of the roof and slide down the other. The raised crimps that ran down the tin roof made it perfect for sliding. This was not an approved activity because there was always the possibility of breaking an arm or a leg, so I never did it more than once or twice. When I didn't get caught, I thought I had outsmarted everyone and gotten away with something. But surely they always knew; what else could have made those tracks in the snow on the roof?

The rest of the morning was spent building a fort. I would roll the snow into huge snowballs, some so big that I could barely roll them into place. The biggest ones went on the bottom. Smaller balls were piled on top. As I used up the snow near the fort, I'd pile rolled snowballs on the sled and transport them to my building site. When the wind picked up in the late morning, the fort gave protection from its attack. I worked hard and steadily, so when the noon whistle sounded, I was actually a little sweaty and very hungry.

The house seemed too warm, but smelled, oh, so good—fresh baked bread, tomato soup and steaming hot chocolate. First my snow-encrusted clothes were hung to thaw in the cellar near the monster coal furnace. My mittens sizzled as they were laid to dry on the hot-air vents in the floor. There would be no more fun in the snow until everything was dry—about the time Father came home from work. Then, maybe, he would take me sliding.

After lunch I dragged out the scissors, last summer's Sears catalog and a cardboard box. As the afternoon hours drifted by, the cardboard box became my dream house. I created my own dollhouse and paper dolls from the catalogs. Carefully, I selected just the right furniture and put it in place with flour-and-water paste. In the meantime, my mother worked in the kitchen while she listened to soap operas on the cream-colored Philco radio. The house was warm and secure; all seemed well with the world.

Occasionally I glanced out the window to see how dark it was getting. If it was too dark, there would be no sliding in the road. Then came the familiar sound of my father in the cellarway, stomping snow off his feet. Yes, there was time for one run. I never realized then how tired he must have been after walking two miles home from work through the snow.

The sun had set and the streetlights were on, but a crack of daylight was left on the horizon. I climbed onto my Flexible Flyer and my father pulled me the mile up the reservoir hill. From the top of the hill, our small town looked like a storybook village. The world seemed pure and peaceful. Lights twinkled; smoke curled up from the chimneys and crystals of snow floated gently down to earth.

I sat on the sled, feet in the center, and with a push from behind, we were off. As we soared down the hill, the wind whipped my face, making it hard to keep my eyes open. Too soon we were at the bottom. One run was all we could ever do—the climb up the hill was just too long.

Occasionally, after dinner, there was another special treat—sugar on snow. We packed the roasting pan with snow. Then maple syrup was boiled until it reached the soft-ball stage. When the hot syrup was drizzled over the snow, we had instant hard maple sugar candy. It was a sweet end to a wonderful day.

Snow days were a gift then—and for me, they still are. I still get snow days off because now I teach school. I remember the joy I felt as a child when there was a snow day. I remember how my children smelled of snow and cold when they came in from playing in the snow and it was my turn to have steaming hot chocolate waiting.

I love snow days even more now that my family is grown and flown from the nest. I still marvel at the beauty of newly fallen snow, and I feel snug and comforted by the white blanket. I treat every snow day as a gift, a gift of time: time to do those things that I *want* to do but don't get to do because of all the things I *have* to do. ❖

Just an Old Tin Can

By Fern Reed Yarnick

During my growing-up years in the 1930s, new toys were few and far between. My brothers and I didn't mind, though. We found we could spend many happy hours with old, throw-away tin cans.

Tin cans were just the right size for can-walking. I remember pushing my shoes down onto the thin metal as hard as I could, until the cans stuck fast around each shoe. What fun we had clogging around the neighborhood!

We must have made a terrible racket, yet none of the parents seemed to mind. From the doorways of their homes, they smiled at the parade of tin cans moving down the street. Nowadays this type of behavior would be called "disturbing the peace," but growing up during hard times, fun was where you found it.

Tin cans played a big part at weddings when I was a child, too. My older brother and his friends decided to serenade one couple while having a little fun of their own. Patiently they pounded holes in a dozen or more cans and tied them together with twine. With only the light from the moon to work by, they struggled to complete the project.

When their "gift" was laid out, it stretched for a good five feet or more. While the festivities continued inside the hall, someone was selected as a lookout. Then, working quickly, the boys attached their surprise gift to the back of the getaway car.

With everything in place, we kids found hiding places close by in order to have a ring-side seat. Excitement rose in our breasts as the bride and groom exited and settled into the car. Their goodbyes said, they pulled the car forward with a lurch. The noise of the tin cans dragging behind was deafening.

With a look of half-humor and half-disgust, the groom opened the car door. He knew full well what had happened. Getting the cans untied took quite some time; and he wasn't the least bit impressed that my brother and his friends had worked so hard.

It wasn't easy to stifle our laughter. The younger kids couldn't keep their composure, and invariably, some of the culprits were caught. The rest of us ran off in all directions. For days, the wedding and the prank we had played were the talk of the neighborhood.

We also used old tin cans to play tin-can alley; other kids called the game kick-the-can. As I remember, only three things were needed to play it: an empty can, a stick and the ability to run like the wind.

The rules were simple. You placed the can near a streetlight. (The game was played at night, making it difficult to find—let alone capture—anyone.) Someone was chosen to be "it." How they were chosen I don't recall; I just remember that they had their hands full. It was a simple cat-and-mouse approach, to catch as many kids as possible.

Many times I was caught off-guard and felt the jab of the stick in my side that meant I was now a prisoner. As each child was captured, he or she joined the growing number of prisoners near the can. No one could leave the spot unless someone paid the fine.

Then it happened … while the cat left home base to capture the rest of the mice, the can stood momentarily unguarded, now fair game. I can still picture one of the freebies streaking toward home base. As our benefactor kicked the can, it sailed out into the field. We prisoners shouted for joy and ran in all directions. We were free!

I am sure this game was played in many different ways. I will never forget what fun we kids had playing for hours with nothing more than an old tin can.

In an age when children must have the latest toy, I sigh and remember how innocent my brothers and I were. Someone has said, "Never look back." Ah, but when you do, you realize that *those* were the Good Old Days. ❖

Junk For Joy

By Venus Bardanouve

We had toys—dolls, sleds, blocks, scooters, balls, etc.—when I was a child, but the things we enjoyed most usually involved some piece of "junk" that didn't cost a penny. I remember the "beautiful" pieces of broken glass or china that we treasured for use as "throwers" in hopscotch games drawn with chalk on the sidewalk or with a stick in the dirt. We stored these glass treasures carefully in cigar boxes, and used them to trade for someone else's treasures.

Nothing surpassed wooden spools. I can still taste the soap from blowing bubbles with a spool. We put a bar of soap in a small dish and sloshed it around to make thick suds. After dipping one end of the spool into the liquid and being sure a film of soapy water covered the hole, we gently blew into the other end and were rewarded with a beautiful bubble.

Boys notched the edges of spools to make them into "tractors." A rubber band was threaded through the spool hole and held in place on one end by a piece of matchstick and on the other end by a headless match. This served as the crank to wind it up and set the tractor in motion.

Spools were also useful for making doll furniture. Little pillows could be put on small ones to make stools, and a piece of cardboard on top of a large spool made a table.

Cans were great not only for kick-the-can, but also for walking. Two medium-size cans were turned upside down. Two holes, one opposite the other, were punched in the sides of each with a hammer and nail. Then a strong string was threaded through the holes and the string ends from each can were tied together about waist high. We then stepped on the cans carefully, held the "reins" tightly in each hand and tramped around the yard in great satisfaction.

Of course, one could graduate to real stilts when someone found two old 2-by-4s and a block of wood that could be cut into wedges to nail onto the 2-by-4s for footholds. The art of walking on these took some time to perfect; usually you started on small stilts or cans.

We made a telephone with a long string and two cans, one attached to each end. You could surely hear your friend's voice from around the corner of the house—if the caller shouted clearly.

And those out-of-date catalogs! We cut out the best-looking heads of a woman, man and children for our families, making a long tab below the head. Then we clothed our little family in coats, hats, dresses and suits cut from the catalog. A slit was made at the top of each clothing figure so that the head could be inserted.

Sometimes we cut out furniture from the catalog, too, and pasted it in boxes to make houses for our paper dolls. We used old matchboxes for beds and tables. And every used envelope was salvaged to use as a file for each doll and its clothes.

Oatmeal boxes made prized doll cradles that could be covered with scraps of cloth or pieces of wallpaper. The artwork was always attached with a paste of flour and water.

Sticks were one of the more useful play

tools. Many fathers—and some children—perfected the art of making whistles out of small willow branches. After cutting a mouthpiece at one end of a small piece cut from a branch, we moistened the bark, tapped it carefully with the knife, then twisted the bark from the wood. After carving a layer off the top of the stick so that air could pass through, we replaced the bark and it whistled like a bird.

Longer sticks were used for horses. I remember when several neighbor children stabled their "horses" in our grape arbor. No horse was like any other. Some were peeled, some had the bark cut in designs or stripes, and some had interesting knots or other features. But all were grand and galloped around the yard nobly. Much horse-trading took place when we had horses stabled in the grape arbor.

Even though we owned dolls, we sometimes used small sticks for people when we played "house." We dressed our stick dolls in leaves or bits of cloth. These stick families stood up nicely in the soft earth under the yellow rose bushes. If you wanted to mark off their home or a corral for their animals, a fence of small sticks could easily be pounded into the ground.

When the grass was cut, we often raked up the cuttings and used it for walls and partitions for houses. Once my father made me a little haystacker, and we often used it to stack hay for those animals. I can still smell the cut grass that gave us so much fun.

Sitting outdoors on hot summer afternoons, we made great, long dandelion chains from the beheaded stems. Of course, it was necessary to first hold one of the heads under each child's chin to see if he or she "liked butter." If some of the yellow pollen stayed on the chin, then surely that child liked butter.

I'm really not sure what that all signified. Perhaps it was of the same importance as "stamping robins" in the spring. This was done by licking the thumb and stamping it on the opposite palm, then stamping the fist in that palm also, calling out the total of robins "stamped" so far that spring. White horses were counted in the same fashion, except the first finger was used.

Hollyhock dolls were another joy of the yard. With skirts made of a large, upside-down hollyhock bloom, a bud head and a small hollyhock hat, they were ready to call on one another. And while we played hollyhock dolls, someone else might be having an air show with parachutes made from men's handkerchiefs tied at the four corners with strings, which were then gathered together in an iron nut. These parachutes were tossed high in the air and sometimes opened as they descended. They might be joined by a sky full of paper airplanes.

String was as good as sticks for making toys. A piece of it could be tied together and slipped over both hands to play cat's cradle. We could remove the string from each other's hands, making intricate patterns.

Buttons joined with string made interesting toys. A button in the middle of a double string was wound up tight by twirling the string with both wrists. We looped the ends of the string over our hands, and when the button was wound tightly enough, we moved our hands back and forth, and the button and string sang as they quickly wound and unwound.

We also enjoyed stringing beautiful necklaces with buttons from our mother's button box. Eventually, though, we had to return the buttons to the box. Those wringers were sure to pop the buttons off of someone's clothes next wash day, and she needed every button for repairs.

Then there were things to roll. Everyone could find an old tire; a brave child might even curl up inside it and let a trusted friend roll it. Our parents told of rolling hoops when they were young, so if we found an iron hoop, we sometimes made a cross of some thin boards and introduced our friends to an "old-fashioned" pastime.

Old wheels ended up on a cart, car or wagon, however wobbly. We used these vehicles as racecars, covered wagons, or just as a way to haul plain dirt or other valuables until the unreliably attached wheels fell off.

One girl collected bottles of various sizes and shapes and made a great-sounding xylophone. That instrument was accompanied by a cigar-box banjo, made with rubber bands stretched on a small board attached to the box.

We fashioned slingshots from Y-shaped sticks and bands cut from old inner tubes. Those inner tubes were most prized, however, for floating on rivers and lakes when we went on picnics. Only hopelessly useless ones were sacrificed for slingshots.

A tent made of blankets hung over the clothesline and weighted down at the edges was good for a whole afternoon of play. Our "meals" while "camping in the tent" were mud pies and similar concoctions. On rainy days, sheets or blankets pinned together and hung over the round oak dining-room table made good tents, and made our mothers happy too. However, when the rain was over, we were outside wading in puddles and sailing flat boats, sometimes with wooden masts sporting paper or cloth sails. Some children attached strings to their boats and pulled the vessels along behind

them. Others urged them along with sticks. Giant leaves also made temporary sailing ships.

Some children became adept at making kites from small sticks and newspapers. Tails made with scraps from Mother's ragbag added a decorative touch. It was thrilling to fly those kites, but making them was almost more fun.

If we had an old jackknife—usually one junked by a dad because a blade was broken—we played "mumblety peg" by tossing the knife blade from each finger. Then we balanced it on our wrists, elbows, shoulders and on until we finally came to the climax of throwing the knife over our heads, called "over the world."

Of course, we played jacks, marbles, ball, cards and many other games that required purchased equipment. But the happiest times I remember were spent creatively using worthless items or other people's junk for our joy. My memories hold true; the best things in life are free. ❖

Hollyhock Dolls

By Marilyn J. Smith

Whenever I see a hollyhock plant, it brings back such sweet memories. When I was a child, playing outdoors was the best thing we could do. We had a wonderful yard filled with flowers and shade trees and the alley behind our house was just bursting with blooming hollyhocks. They grew there like weeds; in fact, my folks called them "barnyard orchids." We could pick all we wanted, and we spent hours playing with the hollyhock dolls we made.

Here's how to make a hollyhock doll: Pull off a flower and a good rounded bud close to the stem. Insert a toothpick up through

the flower for a neck and stick the bud on top for a head. Another toothpick poked crosswise through the top of the flower formed her arms. Then we could decorate or "dress" the dolls with other flowers and leaves. The blossoms from our four-o'clock plants made wonderful bonnets of beautiful colors.

Our hollyhock dolls' gowns ranged in color from white, pale yellow and every shade of pink to deep magenta.

We had lines of waltzing ladies and beautiful ballerinas, and held many fashion shows. I don't know if little girls today ever occupy themselves this way, but it was great fun for us in the 1940s. ❖

The Tarzan Tree

By J.K. Reder

There was a big old tree in the vacant lot by our house that all the kids played on. It was *humungous*. Someone had fastened a thick cable onto a huge branch that grew straight out from the trunk, about 10 feet above the ground—too high for us kids to jump up and grab.

The cable had been bent into a hook at the end, just right to put your foot in. This was back in the 1930s and '40s and all of us kids were crazy about *Tarzan and the Apes*. We went around thumping our chests and giving that wild Tarzan call until our mothers protested, "Stop it! You're driving me out of my mind!"

All summer long, when we didn't have anything to do, and were sick of playing Monopoly, we'd tell our moms, "We're going over to play on the tree."

"OK," they always said, "but be home in time for dinner." They never worried about us. They knew we'd look out for each other.

By the time we got there, 15 or 20 kids had already arrived—big kids, little kids, boys and girls. It didn't make any difference. Usually there was a big kid up in the crotch of the tree to help the smaller ones up. He'd reach down and grab their hand and pull them up until they could get a leg over the branch.

Perched all along that branch were kids waiting their turns. Finally, the one at the head of the line jumped, leaping off into space, then plunged down with an ear-splitting Tarzan yell, and swung on the cable in a wide arc, way out over the cockleburs and crabgrass that covered the sand lot. Eventually, "the old cat died," and "Tarzan" would free his foot, grab the cable and fling it up as hard as he could for the next person.

Such freedom! Such exhilaration! We imagined we were swinging on a vine in the jungles of Africa, just like Tarzan.

How many times we climbed that old tree and got to swing depended on what time we got there and how many kids came. Nobody went home without having a turn. There were never any fights, nor was there any supervision. And come five o'clock, everybody left and went home for supper.

But sure as shootin', you knew that when the sun got high in the sky the next day, kids from blocks around all over the neighborhood would be heading for the Tarzan tree. And you know what? It didn't cost anybody a dime! ❖

Homemade Fun

By Marie McKee

Our mother worked in other people's homes for low wages, so there wasn't much money for buying playthings. The few store-bought toys we owned were mostly Christmas gifts from older sisters. But my twin and I created our own enjoyable homemade toys.

My earliest recollection of homemade fun was playing with what we called "bobby dough."

One bread-baking day when we were 3 years old, a boy of our age came to visit. Our kitchen was rather small, with a big, black cookstove taking up a lot of space. To keep us from getting underfoot, my mother gave each of us a small piece of dough. Three wooden chairs served us our worktables. We made small biscuits that were baked hard and looked like marbles.

From then on, we looked forward to baking day, and eventually made other shapes with the dough. It was our big pleasure during our preschool years. Many years later, I learned that "bobby dough" was named after the boy, Bobby Wren, who had visited us on that bread-baking day.

Our first writing paper was a Pillsbury Cookbook. I still have this deteriorating, 80-year-old book with uneven circles and shapes still visible on its pages. After we learned to write, we had thick tablets with red covers bearing the picture of an Indian's head. We were supposed to use both sides of the paper, but I didn't like to do that. I was scolded many times for not doing so.

I liked to cut out Campbell soup ads from magazines that people gave us. There was a cute jingle under the pictures of the twin boy and girl and I collected them.

We didn't have a desk to write on. But a large adjustable chair with my mother's large breadboard resting across the wooden armrests served as a desktop. The two of us could sit side by side in that chair for some years, drawing and writing. Our school crayons were used only occasionally during summer vacation, as they were kept to be used from one grade to another. But our school paints could be replaced for just 2 cents per cake of color, and so we did more painting than coloring.

I liked to cut out Campbell soup ads from magazines that people gave us. There was a cute jingle under the pictures of the twin boy and girl and I collected them.

My mother showed us how to make a book from tablet paper by sewing down the center fold of the paper. After a few stitches, I had my first scrapbook. We also were shown how to make paste out of flour and water. After pasting the Campbell soup ads in my book, I still had pages for adding my own jingles and poems.

I was in my teens before I had a ready-made scrapbook; I filled it with scenic pictures from neighbors' Sunday papers. Later I tore out the pictures and

A snap, a dash,
A score, a riot —
All thanks to Campbell's
In my diet!

There's health

in the ring of their laughter

21 kinds to
choose from...

Asparagus
Bean
Beef
Bouillon
Celery
Chicken
Chicken-Gumbo
Clam Chowder
Consomme
Julienne
Mock Turtle
Mulligatawny
Mutton
Ox Tail
Pea
Pepper Pot
Printanier
Tomato
Tomato-Okra
Vegetable
Vegetable-Beef
Vermicelli-Tomato

11 cents a can

LOOK FOR THE
RED-AND-WHITE
LABEL

The tumult and riot that suddenly break loose upstairs may summon you to police duty, but there's a hidden chuckle behind your reproof. For you know that boundless energy and vitality are proofs of the children's glowing health ... Such exuberance and vigor are the deserved rewards of all your care in giving the children wholesome food. No wonder Campbell's Vegetable Soup is such a regular, trusted stand-by in millions of homes. For children require plenty of fine garden vegetables for proper growth ... and they get them in extraordinary abundance in this soup which they devour so eagerly. It's a great help to any mother always to have in the home such a richly healthful vegetable food that is so easily prepared and served. And how the children love it! Order it today.

MEAL-PLANNING IS EASIER WITH DAILY CHOICES FROM CAMPBELL'S 21 SOUPS

put in newspaper clippings about weddings, deaths, births, etc. I still have my scrapbooks; they have yellowed with age and some of the clippings are nearly 70 years old.

By the time I was in first grade, I had learned to cut out a simple doll dress and sew it together with a few stitches. My mother made all our clothes, so there were plenty of fabric scraps. I sewed a collection of doll clothes that were the envy of all my friends. Small jointed celluloid dolls were popular then, and I was never without one to sew for. It was exciting to buy a new doll for a small amount when an old one couldn't be mended. My last doll was a larger doll, and I made enough clothes for it to fill a small cedar chest.

Since having a real dollhouse wasn't possible, I made my own from a cardboard box from the grocery store. I used empty spools, small pieces of wood and small boxes to make furniture; more material from the scrap bag gave me curtains and bedding. Someone gave my mother tiny rugs that looked like Oriental rugs and they were used to cover some of the floors. It made a very nice dollhouse to play with.

My mother showed us how to make a doll cradle out of a large oatmeal box by cutting an opening in the side of the box. With some more scrap fabrics for bedding, it made a nice bed for our small dolls.

We were given books for Christmas, so over the years, we acquired a small collection of them, mostly Bobbsey Twin books. Many a rainy summer day, we played library in our front hall on the steps with our friends. The steps were our bookshelves and we numbered our books just like regular library books. When we were old enough to go to a branch library, we spent many hours selecting and reading books.

Our home had coal- and wood-burning stoves and we always needed kindling to start the fires. For a few years, my mother bought scrap lumber from a lumber store. These small pieces of clean wood came in shapes of all kinds; they were just right for building blocks. That was good fun during the winter; we played with the blocks until they were needed for the stoves.

My mother had a big box of buttons, most of which had been cut off of clothing. There was a large variety of sizes, colors and shapes. My twin and I spent many hours pairing the buttons, selecting the prettiest, biggest, etc. Today's children play with costly computer buttons—but we played with salvaged buttons from coats and dresses that cost us nothing.

In our old set of encyclopedias, my twin and I found many pages of exercises. In the evenings, when we still had some energy left, we had fun trying to do them. We worked at them until we were tired enough to go to bed.

We also liked to play with paper dolls that we cut from Sears catalogs. Tiring of misfit clothes, I made new clothes from tablet paper, coloring them with crayons or school paints. Some years the Sunday paper printed paper dolls and a few clothes to color.

One of the games we received from our sisters one Christmas was Uncle Wiggly. On cold winter nights, we would sit on the floor near the stove and play the game many times over. When I wanted a new game, I made one from cardboard, drawing pictures on it to make it interesting. We used buttons as playing pieces, and enjoyed playing it near the warm stove, too.

For years, the most fun we had during school vacations was making a playhouse in our old unpainted woodshed. It was a storage spot for a variety of things, mostly wood to be burned in our stoves. We worked for days cleaning the shed and used some of the wood crates and pieces of lumber to make furniture. On hot days we played in there to escape the summer heat. It was fun to dress up in old dresses, hats and high-heeled shoes, and have "tea parties" of crackers and water. But only once did my friend Elsie and I try to sleep in our playhouse. The noise in the alley frightened us, so we didn't get much sleep.

In the summer, we played store. Gathering the empty cans, boxes and other things to furnish the store was actually the best part. We gathered weeds to use as fresh vegetables. Our money was made from paper and our cash register was a box. We never kept things from one summer to the next, but always gathered up new materials.

My mother used a wagon to carry groceries home from the store. That same wagon was used to carry the bushel baskets of clothing that she washed and ironed for other people. But we did get to play with the wagon, too, coasting down our alley. We shared, taking turns with our friends, as we were the only ones with a wagon.

Grass wasn't kept cut as short as it is today, and there were always plenty of long-stemmed dandelions and clover in our yard. We fitted the dandelion stems together to make necklaces, bracelets and belts, and we braided the long stems of clover into pretend jewelry and headbands.

When the two big catalpa trees were in bloom, we would run up and down our terrace trying to catch the blossoms before they reached the ground. If they didn't fall fast enough, we would throw something up into the branches so that we could continue our game. Those trees also provided us with a shady spot where we could lie on a blanket and talk and dream about our futures. For a while, there was a wooden swing between the trees for us to enjoy.

During my grade-school days, the Friendly House offered sewing lessons for girls and woodworking for boys. Girls made bedding for a doll bed and received a doll if they completed their project. I already knew how to sew, and was showing off to make the girls laugh. I didn't get a doll because I didn't finish the bedding!

One drugstore gave a five-cent credit when you took in sales slips amounting to $5. It took awhile to save $10 worth of slips so that my twin and I could have the fun of selecting five cents worth of penny candy. Those were happy days, selecting jawbreakers, licorice (both black and brown), drops of candy on narrow strips of paper, root beer barrels, tiny chocolate dolls, small, chewy, black dolls, peppermint sticks and much more. Grab bags were filled with small pieces of candy and sometimes, stale popcorn. Cracker Jacks with little prizes were exciting, too.

Boys sometimes lost marbles on the streets and sidewalks, and I started collecting the ones I found. My mother would find them, too. I was given a carrying case called a Charleston Bag and I filled it with more than 100 pretty marbles in all sizes and colors. My friends and I tried playing games with the marbles, but it wasn't our kind of game.

Part of the fun we had as children involved playing games on the street corners after supper. A large group of us would gather under the streetlights in the evening to play Pussy Wants a Corner and Run, Sheep, Run. There wasn't much traffic then and no speeding cars, so we were safe. Nine o'clock came too fast. We hated to leave for home, but we were punished if we didn't come when we were called.

Someone showed us how to mix Ivory soap and water so that we could blow bubbles through the hole in an empty spool. We did that often and generously supplied our friends with soap until our mother stopped us. In school, we had art lessons on how to carve animals out of a bar of Ivory soap. We used our soap animals to wash with, as usual.

My twin and I had simple birthday parties that included a big cake and a few 10-cent prizes for winners of the party games. Quite a few of our gifts were pretty handkerchiefs. We appreciated them then, but today's children wouldn't care for that kind of gift.

For a few years, we had fun trying to play "tennis" in our small yard, hitting a small rubber ball back and forth with 25-cent rackets. We didn't have a net, but we were real proud of our inexpensive rackets.

By the time we neared our teen years, cars were getting more plentiful. That gave us the idea of making a pretend car. We laboriously carried a long, heavy workbench from our garage to a grassy area beside our house. Using old oilcloths that had once covered our kitchen table, we covered the side so the rain couldn't get in. Someone found a wheel from an old wagon, and with a stick to hold it up, we had a steering wheel. Small wooden boxes served as our seats. We didn't know about brakes and gear shifts then, so we just turned the wheel to take off on our pretend journeys. We spent many happy hours traveling on imaginary trips in our "car."

Our playthings were very valuable to us. They meant much to us because we enjoyed being creative, and we loved every minute of our play. ❖

The Games We Played

Chapter Two

Games were at the center of much of the fun we had back in the Good Old Days. Whether they were well known games like horseshoes or baseball, or the kind you make up as you go, we never lacked for plenty of ways to play together.

Rainy days were always a challenge to our world of games, particularly for us rough and tumble boys. Ball games would have been even more fun with mud on the field, but most mothers didn't view it that way, so they were out of the question. We had wooden floors, but I again figured Mama wouldn't like us playing Mumblety Peg on them with our pocketknives. Even *girls* couldn't play hopscotch or jump rope on such dreary days.

I envied kids whose homes had attics. There was always some interesting game to play in an attic. One of my best friends, Steve, had a home blessed with one, and there was no end to what attic games we could invent there on a rainy day.

One trunk in the upper sanctuary yielded a couple of old military uniforms and we pretended we were soldiers protecting the home front from invasion. That game became too bland pretty quickly, since we were on the same side. So we chose sides (easy to do since there was only two of us) and our war game escalated until Steve's mother insisted on a cease fire.

When the girls joined us, we could pretend we were pioneers, setting up housekeeping on the Great Plains. Trunks and valises became covered wagons or maybe the walls of a frontier fort. The girls found fancy hats, dresses and shoes and suddenly the game setting changed to the big city—maybe Boston or New York City. We were sophisticates (quite a stretch for country bumpkins and small town imps) out for a stroll along the boardwalk.

In one suitcase we found old school books, McGuffey Readers from the 19th century and some other elementary primers. We played school, with one of the girls taking on the role of the marm. She dutifully led our "class" in readin', 'ritin' and 'rithmetic. As always, I excelled in recess when we got to that part of the lesson.

After that, we spun tops, pitched pennies and played Pick-Up Stix. Finally we retired to an old quilt-covered settee and worked on crossword puzzles, waiting out the rain and gloom.

The next day was bright as a new dime. We boys could pretty much go back to ignoring the girls. We returned to baseball, Mumblety Peg and swinging Tarzan-style from a rope in our favorite climbing tree. The girls went back to jacks, jump-rope and hopscotch.

Our games in the Good Old Days taught us a lot about giving and sharing, cooperation and teamwork. Whether it was up in Steve's attic or out on the ball field in the bright sunlight, we were molded by them. Inside or out, parlor or playground, we learned a lot from the games we played.

—Ken Tate

After Dinner at the Farm by John Falter © 1948 SEPS: Licensed by Curtis Publishing

Champion Checker Player

By Virginia Hearn Machir

In the 1920s we didn't have television or radio. On cold, blustery winter nights when the snow was blowing, we amused ourselves playing Old Maid, Authors, Chinese checkers, dominoes and checkers.

Helen, Janet, Doris and I would often sit on the linoleum near the black iron wood-burning stove, engaged in an argumentative game of Old Maid. The kerosene lamp put out a rosy glow from the library table, and a huge bowl of popcorn waited to be devoured.

At the same time, Mom and Dad would be engaged in a serious game of checkers at the library table. They sat silently, plotting each move slowly, carefully guarding "king row," jumping with chuckles and crowning their opponent's king with reluctance.

Suddenly we would hear Mom exclaim, "Ha, ha, Dan, I beat you again!"

The next night or two, Dad would suggest they play dominoes because he could beat Mom at this game. Then, after two or three nights of dominoes, with Dad being the winner, he would regain his confidence and suggest they have a game of checkers.

But it was the same old story time after time, with Dad losing and Mom boasting gleefully, "Crown my king, Dan. Ha, ha! I beat you again."

When we had company, Dad would bring out the checkerboard and ask the visitors to be Mom's opponent, hoping they would beat her. She never lost a game. She was truly a champion checker player, but a boastful winner. When Dad won at dominoes he never crowed about it.

But Dad never gave up the idea that he might win a game of checkers from Mom. Again and again they played, and as usual Mom would win with her crowing, "Ha, ha, I won again!"

One wintry night we children were seated on the floor, playing a game of Authors, and Mom and Dad were playing yet another game of checkers. Suddenly we heard Mom's familiar boastful, "Ha, ha, I won!"

Dad jumped up from the table, raked all the checkers off the board into their box, strode over to the wood-burning stove, opened the door and threw the checkers, box and all, into the fire. Then he rushed back to the table, grabbed the checkerboard, gave it a whack across his knee and broke it in half, opened the stove door and threw it into the fire too. Mom just sat there, speechless.

"Now you'll never win another danged checker game from me!" Dad exclaimed.

We children just sat there, wide-eyed. We couldn't believe our eyes. Then suddenly we were struck with a fit of giggles, and Helen and I went into the kitchen with the excuse of getting a drink of water. We whispered and giggled together; we thought it was very funny that Dad had burned the checker game, but were certain that he wouldn't think it was funny at that particular time.

Dad lost his checker champion mate almost 30 years ago. We kid him and ask him if he remembers the night he burned the checker game. He just grins sheepishly and answers, "Maggie sure was a good checker player!" ❖

Jack, the Knife

By Alan Sanderson

Where I lived back in the 1930s, nearly every growing boy had his own jackknife. Usually it had two sturdy blades. The blades were set in a variety of casings; mine had been molded in the shape of the letter "S" leaning forward, and sported a bright green strip of plastic between the two steel ends on each side. Far removed from even the connotation of today's switchblades, our knives were always used in a positive sense, whether at work or play.

Unless it happened to be money, there was nothing more valuable I carried in my pocket.

After I finished my household chores, I had "work" of my own to do. If I was by myself, I might decide to carve my initials along with those of my latest love on a convenient scrub oak tree. Or perhaps I would sit on the back steps and try to fashion a gun from an old piece of wood that had been lying around in the yard.

Sometimes I'd search for a long, straight branch that possessed the snapping strength I desired. When all of my specifications had been met, I'd sever my choice from the large bush or sapling and slice the bark and twigs from it. Then I'd drive a nail through the bottom of a clean, topless tin can and secure it on one end of my stick to form a hand guard for my new sword. In those Depression days, we had to make a good many of our toys or go without, as few parents had money to buy them.

On days that I was with my pals, we'd frequently elect to fix the "shack" in which we could play cards, shielded from the sun. Just across from my house amongst a group of trees were several rectangular slabs of stone that had long ago been discarded. They made dandy seats for us. All that we needed was a good roof. Of course, at the beginning of every summer, we'd start off by constructing it.

Out would come our knives to trim a dozen or more tree limbs that someone's hatchet had brought down. One of these makeshift poles was pounded into the ground at each of the four corners. Lengths of rope were then cut to tie these to another set of four poles laid horizontally across the top. Any poles that were left served as "rafters" to support the foliage we gathered. Naturally, these leaves needed to be replaced every few days.

But all work and no play would've made my "Jack" dull. My earliest recollection of a game using a knife was Mumblety Peg, the one in which the point of the blade was held on various parts of the body such as the fingers, elbow, shoulder, head, knees, etc., and flipped toward the ground. If it stuck in the soil, the player went on to the next spot in the series. Otherwise, the knife was passed to the next player.

A second innovation was to lay the knife vertically against the palm of the left hand while kneeling on the grass and then catapult it over the right, resting in the form of a hurdle. The idea was to see who could get the knife to land upright the most consecutive tries.

I wasn't interested in playing these two games much, however, the main reason being that the participants were usually girls.

Jackknife baseball was what really quickened my interest. One afternoon when the sky blackened and a discouraging downpour was practically certain, a friend of mine suggested I bring a wide, thin board onto his screened porch. While the rain hissed down, we both sat there cross-legged on the floor with the board between us, and he explained the rules. Two blades had to be used, but the secondary one was only pulled out halfway. He spun the knife end over end to demonstrate the best way of getting it to stick in the wood.

Misses were "outs." When they totaled three,

that player's half of the inning was over. Causing the knife to stand erect on only the main blade constituted a home run; if it was supported in the board by the smaller blade, that was a triple. A two-base hit was accorded the "batter" when the short blade scored by itself, inducing the knife to stand like the letter "T." The most common hit, a single, came about when the base of the knife landed on the board simultaneously with the second blade. This stance made the main part of the knife appear to be an inverted "V."

Our interest never flagged because we always had to keep track of the men on base and how far they could move up on each hit. I always tried to be the home team so that I could have last bats. Then, if I could stage a big rally in my final turn, there could be no retaliation from my opponent.

But my favorite jackknife game had to be enjoyed far from the watchful eyes of our ever-alert mothers. Had they witnessed our antics, I'm sure they would have raised some objections.

A steady foursome of us generally avoided this by informing our parents that we were going on a hike. We did, too, laden down with tasty tuna-fish salad or marshmallow fluff–and–jelly sandwiches, strawberry soda, the essential bottle opener and our jackknives.

Approximately a mile from where we lived was a sheltered spot in the fringe of woods we called, for obvious reasons, "the pines." Here and there on the many small, brown-needled slopes were some handy boulders, any one of which could serve as a natural table. An extra bonus was the gurgling brook that we used to refrigerate our drinks.

After the eating came the game. Actually, it was mostly a variation of baseball. A home run was translated into a hundred points; a triple, 75; a double, 50; and a single, 25 points. The object was to avoid being the last to score at least 500. As long as the jackknife stayed in the ground on one, two or both blades at the end of each somersault, the player whose turn it was had the chance to add to his total. An unsuccessful flip turned the knife immediately over to the next boy—unless he wanted to "risk it." This meant an extra turn, but if another consecutive miss occurred, all the previous points earned were forfeited and that particular player would have to start again from zero when his turn came around again. Still, everyone "risked it." This was part of the excitement of the game, and not to do so would have labeled that fella a "sissy" in front of his pals.

Out of the suspense came the real fun—that is, if you didn't happen to be the unfortunate who didn't reach 500. This unlucky guy had to pay the penalty of "pulling the peg." A soft, muddy spot down by the swift brook was usually selected for this ritual. The champ of the round would find a sliver of wood about 3 inches long and, in three whacks, hammer it as far into the ground as he could with the butt of the knife. The second of us to reach the magic figure would then administer his three blows and so on until we all had had our lusty swings.

The luckless loser would then have to lie on his stomach and pull out the peg with his teeth, with no help from his hands. Needless to say, the peg was often buried beneath the surface. In addition to getting a good taste of Mother Earth, one had to be careful that a bug or worm didn't enrich this "dessert."

As distasteful as this might have been to our moms and dads, we didn't hurt anyone and each of us had an opportunity to laugh, and what's so bad about that? In those days, the jackknife was a positive possession—not a deadly weapon! ❖

© *Sweet Victory* by Jim Daly

Street Games

By Richard P. Borkowski

After hearing what it costs a boy to play baseball today, my mind shifted back to a well-worn cobblestone street along the Delaware River in Philadelphia. Back then we played all kinds of sports and games all day long (and all night, if the street lamps worked) without it costing our parents or us one penny.

A worn-out broom was quickly converted into a baseball bat, a three-inch piece of rubber garden hose served as the baseball, and a small, rolled-up notebook was the official street football. Anytime a game called for a real ball, someone would plead with the janitor of a nearby warehouse to "see if there were any old balls on the roof." Somehow, there was always one up there. That roof was our own athletic equipment center.

I never realized it then, but we sure saved our parents a lot of money. Take, for example, the savings on travel expenses. We never had to travel from one field to another. The widest, least traveled street with a lot of natural boundary lines (like curbs, lamp posts and trees) was our baseball diamond—and our basketball court, and our football field. If we needed a home plate, someone found a brick or loose cobblestone. Bases ranged from broken curbs to ice wagons. The gutters served as our sidelines for football, and any unusually marked area on a wall was our basketball hoop.

The greatest savings to our parents, however, was in the area of coaches and umpires. Who needed a guy with a master's degree in physical education to teach us games? We had our own list of official games to fit any terrain or situation—like the day one of those troublesome automobiles broke down around second base. We formed a quick huddle, and the car became second base for the day.

Our means for deciding any close play was perfect: The biggest guy made the final ruling on all questionable calls, and the game played on. I wonder if the crews of officials who work each modern pro football game are any improvement over our system?

Each of our street games was full of traditions and customs. We never broke the unwritten policies of game selection. "Hey, how about halfball today?" someone shouted.

"No sir—let's play hoseball!"

"We played that yesterday! Today it's stickball."

After everyone mentioned another dozen games apiece, they paused and looked to the biggest guy present. "Today," he announced, "we will start off with hoseball!"

Naturally, the guy who owned a piece of equipment had a say in the game selection, especially if he threatened to take his stuff and go home, or to another street.

The next order of business was choosing up sides. The two best players flipped anything that had one side you could call "heads" and another you could call "tails." Sometimes it was even a coin. The winner was permitted first choice. Pitching a stone to see who was closest to a line, or shooting out fingers to win your choice of odd or even were other means of drafting teams.

My favorite way of choosing up was tossing the stick. Each captain attempted to place his hand at the top by alternating hand grasps with his opponent after one tossed the stick to the other. What a contest of strategy and hand

My favorite way of choosing up was tossing the stick. Each captain attempted to place his hand at the top by alternating hand grasps with his opponent after one tossed the stick to the other.

squeezing to get your hand at the very top! Whoever succeeded then had to twirl it around his head three times without dropping it. Next, he held it at arm's length while the other tried to kick it out of his hand.

If he survived all that, he got first choice.

The ground rules also had to be discussed. "A hit past the lamp post is a single, anything past the car is a double. Jack's step is a triple, and anything past the corner on a fly is a homer."

The only unbreakable, almost holy rule on our street concerned the games you could and could not play during certain times of the year. Spring and summer meant baseball only. Fall was football, and winter was either basketball or hockey. Of course, we seldom played the official versions of these games, and no one really knew when one season officially ended and the next began. It always worked out, though. It had something to do with the biggest guy again.

Baseball on the Philadelphia streets really meant hoseball, or Philadelphia stickball, or mushball, or halfball. Sometimes we'd play hoseball for a month straight. Another time we'd play the entire series of summer games in a single day.

Hoseball was my game. Cut the broom off the broomstick to make a bat. Find an old garden hose and cut it into three-inch pieces for balls. (Our neighborhood always seemed to have short water hoses.)

The rules were close to those for baseball except that you didn't have to run after hitting the ball. That's what I liked about hoseball; if you hit it a certain distance and it wasn't caught, it was automatically a single, a double, and so forth.

The only people that didn't like hoseball were the families that owned windows.

Philly stickball was the most popular because it was the closest to real baseball and it made everyone feel rich—we had to use a real ball. A broomstick, a ball, four bricks for the bases and it was play ball all day—or until the ball broke.

I've since tried to establish the difference between Philly stickball and stickball played in New York. So far, the only difference seems to be that one was played on Philadelphia streets and the other on New York streets.

The hardest part of my childhood was trying to hit a knuckle-curve-spitter applied to a dead ball with a broomstick.

Mushball was always played after stickball. When the ball was really, really dead and starting to rip, we'd stuff it with old rags and paper and wrap it with some black tape. Stickball now became mushball.

When the mushball started to break, it was time for the game every pitcher loved—halfball. The Wright brothers must have pitched halfball prior to their great discovery.

Halfball is just like hoseball, except that a half of a ball was pitched. This half moon was the remains of the mushball, which had once been a stickball. A halfball pitched underhand looks like a soft, miniature Frisbee flipping and flopping to the tune of every known air current. It can drop five feet over the plate, or rise two stories.

In the fall, the game was football. To be specific, it was assignment-book football. (Who could afford a real football?) It seems that long ago in the folklore of our neighborhood, a boy wanted to play football so badly that he made the supreme sacrifice by rolling up his small school assignment book and wrapped it with a rubber band, and assignment-book football was born.

The game is like touch football without a football. Oh, those long pass patterns down the curb … a fake at the ice wagon … in and out of the vacant lot … and a great one-hand catch for six points! What hidden-ball tricks, corner-to-corner passes, and what arguments about whether he tagged him with one hand or two! The height of skill was to punt the four-inch assignment book on fourth down.

When winter arrived, the street became a hockey-basketball arena. If it snowed we played tin-can hockey for about a week straight, after clearing the snow. Another time it was our version of basketball that we called ledgeball.

Tin-can hockey was played with or without sticks, and with or without a tin can. If a can couldn't be found, we substituted a rock, a half-ball or someone's sneaker (but never the biggest guy's sneaker). Nevertheless, the game was still called tin-can hockey. If you didn't have a stick, you used your foot.

Now hitting a bent tin can with your foot isn't so bad, but those face-offs with an opponent's stick was tough. As the sticks broke, the game looked more like soccer, but it was still called tin-can hockey.

Ledgeball became part of our street schedule when Fatty Plotski discovered "the ledge," a small overhang above the warehouse garage doors. If you could shoot the basketball (usually a three-inch bouncy ball found on the roof) so that it struck the top side of the ledge, it was a field goal. Foul shots were only granted in cases of blood. Ever try to dribble a three-inch ball on cobblestones, up a curb, shoot at a foot-long ledge, and try to avoid meeting a garage door? Ledgeball was never a polished game, but it was exciting.

There were many other minor-league street games like Buck-Buck, Box Ball, Sidewalk Tennis, Bottle-Top Golf and Blood Alley, but they were played when a mother kicked us out on the street, or when the milkman's horse couldn't wait till the next street.

Today the streets are too clogged, too dirty and too unsafe for a return to these games in most big cities. The rules for kids are engraved carefully in official booklets, for all neighborhoods, cities and countries. And a tin can seldom replaces an official hockey puck.

Nevertheless, I'll always remember those simple, cheap, fun games on "our" street, especially when I pass a sporting goods store. Wonder if those stores would even be interested in handling old broomsticks? ❖

Guessing Game by Revere F. Wistehoff © 1927 SEPS: Licensed by Curtis Publishing

Parlor Games

By Harvey Burns

emember when there were "sittin rooms" and parlors—places where friends, beaus and belles went for simple entertainment when there was no television? Whenever a few friends gathered in the evening or after church, there was always time for a few simple but fun parlor games. Here are a few from the book, *Popular Songs & Amusements*, published in 1915.

The Game of Telegrams

Pencils and paper are distributed, and 10 of the players are each asked to give a letter of the alphabet. These letters every player of the party writes in sequence at the top of his or her sheet of paper.

The hostess then announces that everyone is to write a telegram, the 10 words to begin with the 10 letters given, in consecutive order, as:

Letters given: S, A, Q, T, L, N, K, M, B, E.

Telegram: "Send arnica quickly; tell Lizzie nothing; kitten mutilated by expressmen."

Or a subject may be given for all to write on—as an accident, a proposal of marriage, congratulations, condolences or an appointment.

The Game of Broken Quotations

The following has proved excellent for starting an evening of games. The hostess, having prepared half again as many quotations as there are players, each written on a strip of paper and cut in two or more places, pins the slips of paper on curtains, cushions, furniture and picture frames before the guests arrive.

When everyone has come, the purpose of the game is explained in this way: Each player is to find the beginning of a quotation among the slips of paper around the room, and having secured that, is required to find the next piece of it, and the next until he has the whole.

Then he starts with another in the same way. The game goes on until all the quotations have been taken, when the person who has the greatest number receives a prize.

Here are a couple of other games we played when family or friends got together for an evening of frivolity.

The Game of the Five Senses

Each player must be provided with pencil and paper. He is afterward blindfolded, and the hostess proceeds to test him with regard to the five senses. She first tries him with regard to:

Taste—A tray with a dozen or more things to be tasted—sweet, sour, pleasant and disagreeable—is placed before him. Only a tiny taste is needed. The eyes are then unblinded and each player must write down, in order, the names of what he has been tasting. Two party prizes are given for each trial, a first prize and a booby prize, to the two who have given the most correct and incorrect answers.

Smell—A tray is brought in to the blindfolded players, and spices, medicines, flowers and perfumes are offered to them to smell, after which each player notes his sensations.

Hearing—Again the players are blindfolded, while all the other guests assembled in the room assist in testing their sense of hearing. Every kind of noise is made at once—singing, crying, laughing, ringing of bells, pounding, tearing paper and the trial of different voices of well-known friends. A violin, a guitar and banjo may also assist at this test.

Touch—A tray is now brought to the blind-folded players, with a dozen or more articles to be felt by each person in turn. After the blind-folds are removed, each player writes down the objects felt.

Sight—A tray must now be placed before the players—obviously now without blind-folds—and they are to look at the dozen or more objects displayed upon it while 20 is counted slowly. The tray is removed, and the players must note all the objects they can remember.

Prizes may be given for each of the senses separately, or for the five combined.

Mathematical Magic

Remember the math games that were once used at parties? Here is one for determining a girl s age and month of birth. Tell her to put down the number of the month in which she was born, then to multiply it by 2, then to add 5, then to multiply it by 50, then to add her age, then to subtract 365, then to add 115. She then tells the result of her calculation.

The two figures to the right will tell you her age, and the remainder the month of her birth. Example: An answer of 822 means she is 22 years old and was born in the eighth month, August. ❖

Yesterday's Toys

By Nellie Jones

I remember a time before television and computer games, when children depended on their imagination and simple homemade toys for entertainment.

We played "school" with a simple arrange-ment of chairs. There might be some squabbling over who would be teacher, but we usually settled on taking turns.

By merely rearranging the chairs single-file, we could play "train" and quarrel over who d be engineer and conductor.

Placing a plank across chairs for a counter and borrowing some staples from the kitchen cabinet, we created a make-believe store.

Girls learned to make a doll from a clothes-pin and a hollyhock blossom, and to fashion a dollhouse from a cardboard box. We might even talk Mom out of some leftover wallpaper for interior decor.

Boys constructed tractors and other vehicles out of wooden spools, rubber bands and match-sticks. And each had an arsenal of handmade slingshots of various calibers.

On winter evenings we played checkers on boards drawn on cardboard boxes, using bottle caps for checkers.

In summer we wrote and produced "theater" in the barn or garage, changing the plot and cast as necessary to accommodate any neighbor chil-dren who wanted to join.

A beanbag made from sturdy denim and filled with dry beans or peas or corn was a fair sub-stitute for a ball. It didn t bounce, but we could play catch, Annie Over and dodgeball with it.

A discarded auto tire, hung by a strong rope to a low tree branch, became our swing. Dad s help was usually required to make it. But all on our own we devised another use for old tires, not always highly approved by our parents. We curled up inside them and rolled ourselves or each other down a steep hill. Talk about a thrill ride!

The only time we got store-bought toys was at Christmas, but if we were deprived, we didn t know it. And if we dared to utter the word "bored" in our parents hearing we would have been handed a hoe and sent to the melon patch! ❖

Playing Jacks

By Marie Lundgren

I still see jacks in stores today, but I never see girls playing this old game any more. I played jacks from St. Louis, Mo., to Albuquerque, N.M., to Redlands, Calif., and back to St. Louis, until I had a callous on the entire right side of my trusty right hand. We played on smooth blue-and-white tile porches, on marble steps, on stone and slate hearths. The season for jacks ran from about Easter to Halloween, about the same as for jumping rope and hopscotch.

My grandfather was an inveterate golfer and I caddied for him often, making me the proud possessor of a cigar box full of golf balls. I refused to play jacks with any other type of ball, as you needed a good bouncer in order to have time to scoop up a dozen arbitrary jacks.

I m sure many of you ladies in your 60s and 70s remember these variations of jacks:

In the Barn: Throw out the jacks onto the playing surface; make a "barn" of your left hand by curving it and setting the outer edge of it on the playing surface. On one bounce, scoop the jacks into the barn in ones, twos, three, etc., to the 12s.

Plain Jacks: Throw out 12 jacks on playing surface. Bounce the ball and pick up the jacks, one at a time, on each bounce and place in your left hand. If you didn t miss, next throw them up by twos, then by threes, etc., until you pick up all 12. When you miss, the next girl plays, and on your next turn, you start playing where you missed before.

Over the Fence: Place outer side of left hand on playing surface, and as ball bounces once, pick up jacks and lift them over your hand—the "fence"—by ones, twos, threes, and so forth.

Double Bounce: This is the easy one.

Let the ball bounce twice for each play from ones to the 12s.

No Bounce: Throw ball high so you can make your play before it comes down, placing jacks in your left hand as in Plain Jacks.

Pick 'Em Up and Lay 'Em Down: On one bounce, pick up jacks and lay them down on playing surface. Play ones to twelves without throwing them out again.

Around the World: Throw the ball, and before it bounces, pick up jacks, and with them in your right fist, circle the ball in midair with fist and lay them down on playing surface, on one bounce. This is one of the most difficult, especially when you have an audience in a tournament.

Haystacks: On one bounce, place one jack on top of another, and when you have six haystacks, pick up each on one bounce and place in your left hand.

Misses: Dropping jacks, not catching the ball, or touching a jack you are not supposed to touch in a particular game. If you see two jacks touching and you say "Touch!" before another player does, you may separate them and resume your play.

Since jacks are still sold in stores today, maybe we will see a revival of this game of skill and finesse! ❖

Going in Circles

By Janice Barnes

When I look back, it seems that so many of our games involved us children getting in a circle for one activity or another.

Drop the Handkerchief is one of the earliest games I can remember playing. It was, if memory serves me right, on my fourth birthday, at the only birthday party I can remember ever having. (Life out in the country with neighbors a considerable distance away was not conducive to big social events.)

Drop the Hanky by Hal Sutherland, courtesy of Wild Wings Inc.

On this particular time, however, Mama had invited a few kids over for a Sunday afternoon party. Most of those who attended were cousins from Daddy s huge extended family. The main attraction was a couple of hours of games, including Drop the Handkerchief.

We stood with our faces toward the inside of the circle as one of us ran around the outside with handkerchief in hand. He or she dropped it at someone s heels. The one at whose feet it was dropped had to pick it up and give chase, attempting to catch the runner before he could get to the vacant place in the ring.

A couple of years later I remember playing the same game on a rainy day in our small country school. This time the runner would drop the handkerchief upon a desk. The occupant of that desk then had to grab the "hanky" (as we country folk called it) and chase the runner in an attempt to catch him before he got back to the empty desk.

How many of us got our first crack at chasing the opposite sex with this simple game? Many boys probably secretly hoped a certain young lady would drop the handkerchief at his desk. Or when *he* was "it" and dropped the handkerchief at her desk, he then slyly slowed down rounding the bend by the teacher s desk to

allow the girl to catch him.

A variation of Drop the Handkerchief was Have You Seen My Sheep?

In this game the player outside the circle touched someone on the back and asked, "Have you seen my sheep?" The other replied, "How was he dressed?" The first then described the clothing of some player whom, when he recognized himself, had to run around the circle and try to regain his place without being tagged.

Another game we all played in a circle was Blind Man s Bluff. (I have also heard this old game called Blind Man s Buff.)

In it a circle was formed with a blindfolded child in the center. The players forming the circle moved steadily around the one blindfolded until he gave a signal to stop.

The "blind man" then pointed a wand or finger at some part of the circle. The player who happened to be pointed at moved to a position within the circle, and the blindfolded player tried to catch him. If successful, he had to guess who he had caught. If the guess was correct, the one caught became the blind man; otherwise he took his place in the circle again, and the game proceeded as before.

In French Blind Man s Bluff the child pointed at had to answer some question posed by the blind man, who then guessed who answered. If successful, the two exchanged positions, and the game continued.

Another variation of Blind Man s Bluff was Ruth and Jacob. In it, a girl was chosen to be Ruth, or a boy to be Jacob. The one chosen was blindfolded, turned around several times and left in the center of the circle.

If a girl was chosen, she had to step forward and touch some boy, who took his place in the circle. Ruth then called, "Where art thou, Jacob?" and Jacob answered, "Here."

As often as Ruth called, Jacob was required to answer. Guided by his voice, Ruth gave chase. When Jacob was caught, Ruth had to identify him. If she failed, she had to try another boy; if successful, Jacob was blindfolded and chose some girl.

Another blindfold variation we sometimes enjoyed on the playground at school was Still Pond, No More Moving.

In this game one child was blindfolded and placed in the center of the playground while the others scattered about. After a short time the one blindfolded called out, "Still pond, no more moving."

All then had to stand still, or move not more than a certain number of steps, according to the size of the playground. The one blindfolded attempted to catch one of the other players, and when successful had to guess whom he had captured or let him go. If he guessed right, the one caught became "it."

There were many variations of these circle and blindfolding games, and many were adapted easily for play in the schoolroom. ❖

Hopscotch

By Betty Artlip Lawson

I seldom see girls playing hopscotch in our neighborhood. It seems to me a pity that they do not enjoy the game the way we girls did in the 1930s and 40s when I was growing up in Iowa.

It was not a game we took lightly. We devoted several weeks each spring to an unofficial hopscotch tournament. It was played again through the summer months and we had one final tournament in mid-fall, usually just before our hopscotch designs were covered by snow.

For three years I claimed the championship. But at least three other girls felt that they were the top bananas, so you can see that my status as champion would not have stood up to close scrutiny.

When most of the girls agreed that snow was over for the year, every girl in our small town began a diligent search for a piece of leftover chalk. If searching our homes failed to produce this necessary item, we proceeded to the nearest gravel path, driveway or roadway where we searched carefully for just the right sort of gravel: soft enough to leave the desired marks on the sidewalk, but not so soft that the lines could be wiped off simply by stepping on them. Once we found a suitable piece, we hoarded it jealously throughout the spring tournament.

I started practicing with the simple single-double alternate hopscotch drawing. But in another carefully chosen spot on my home s sidewalk, I drew a different, much more complex pattern.

Before accepting a challenge to play a game, a hopscotch player had to attend to at least two important items of business. The first was to select the proper throwing object. When I first began playing hopscotch, I thought any flat pebble was satisfactory. But as the fine points of the game became clearer to me, my standards rose much higher. The last year I was in the running for the town hopscotch championship, I used a portion of a discarded ankle chain, adding or subtracting links from it as the situation warranted.

The second item of business was to be satisfied once and for all that the complex hopscotch pattern one had claimed for her own was the one that would provide every possible advantage for the designer. I wanted my chosen pattern to be very tough for any opponent not familiar with the combination. I then set about practicing on every possible design my mind could think of while still having time to practice on my own pattern.

When my game was the best it could be and my throwing object was performing properly, it was time to wander around and watch a few matches and spy out other patterns, if possible. You might think it was time to hunt up an opponent, but this was not the case. If one were to challenge too quickly, ridicule and/or disappointment might well follow. If the one challenged was not in your league, the audience was quite capable of quietly booing and sneering the hapless challenger. If, on the other hand, one challenged a player who had gone into early training, there was a terrifying chance one might lose the first match and thus forfeit any further bid for the championship.

If a challenger first watched a few matches, chances improved that she would choose a worthy but not-too-superior opponent. But if one insisted on watching too many matches before challenging, she took the chance of losing the advantage of playing at least part of her games on her home pattern. One had to win at least four or five evenly matched games and earn a reputation of sorts before a challenger felt the need to seek you out on your home hopscotch pattern.

For four to eight weeks each year, this fascinating game held the undivided attention of all the girls in the correct age group in our small town. And we did not play just to have something to do; it was serious business for most of us. (Those who claimed not to be serious were usually only pretending unconcern and disinterest. Usually these girls were unskilled in the art; and yet, even most of these practiced secretly on backyard designs until they had improved enough to join in the competition.) This uncomplicated game of skill kept us out of mischief and outside in the healthy sunshine for hours during summer vacation and after school in the spring and fall as well.

And it cost nothing at all. We spent no money for chalk; hence the search for gravel. We were in no one s way, and our games were never unduly noisy or boisterous. If adults needed to use the sidewalk, we politely picked up our throw pieces (remembering exactly where the opponent s piece had been lying, of course), and waited with a smile while they walked past. Then we replaced our throw pieces and resumed our game.

Hopscotch is a memory from my girlhood that I shall always cherish. It taught me much about competition and sportsmanship. It also helped me learn that while practice doesn t always make perfect, it does bring a decided improvement.

My husband and I had one son and one daughter. I taught our daughter the art of hopscotch, and even though she couldn t find as many opponents as I had as a child, she enjoyed the game.

We have been blessed with two grandsons, both much beloved, but now we are expecting another grandchild. If we are blessed with a granddaughter, one of the many things I hope to do is to show her how much fun she can have with a piece of chalk, a stretch of smooth sidewalk and a flat pebble. ❖

The Way We Were by Paula Vaughan © Copyright Newmark USA 1996

Jumping Ropes

By Mary P. Elwell

*D*id you ever jump rope when you were a kid? I did. Have you ever watched a bunch of kids as they jumped into the swinging ropes and have you listened to their special chants for each game of swinging ropes? It s fun to do and fun to watch. Let me attempt to refresh your (and my) memories.

Jump-roping is one of the pleasures of childhood. It is also a great form of exercise. However, jump-roping owes some of its success and popularity to the wonderful rhymes or chants that accompany the jumper and the rope turners. These chants help them keep time to the beat of their feet while the jumper jumps over and under the constantly swinging ropes. I can recall a few chants:

"School, school, the Golden Rule, Sign your name at the bottom of the list."

With this chant, the child jumps into the middle of the swinging ropes which are held by two other kids. As she hops to the sound of the chant, she spells out her name: "C-H-R-I-S-S-Y." With each letter, the rope takes a full swing. If by chance she should trip on the rope, she is out of the game. She then goes to the end of the line and another kid jumps in and attempts to spell her name. As many as six or even more can enjoy this fun game of jumping rope.

Another chant goes like this: "Teddy bear, teddy bear, read the news. Teddy bear, teddy bear, teddy bear turn around. Teddy bear, teddy bear, touch the ground."

In this chant, the kid has to perform each command while the ropes are constantly in swing. Sometimes, this is not easily done and the jumper may lose her step.

Sometimes, a bunch of kids get in a line, about 12 of them. The first kid will jump into the swinging ropes and yell, "Kindergarten!"

Then another kid jumps in and yells, "First grade!"

She jumps out and another jumps in and says, "Second grade!" and so on, until they reach "12th grade!" If one of them trips in the ropes, she must go to the end of the line and begin again.

Here s a real fast one: "Red hot chili peppers, red hot chili peppers, faster, faster, faster, red hot chili peppers, faster faster faster!" Anyone who stumbles has to try again.

Another cute jump-rope chant is: "Cinderella, dressed in yella , went upstairs to kiss her fella. Made a mistake and kissed a snake. How many doctors did it take?"

As the rope is being turned, the jumper counts every full swing: "One! Two! Three! Four!" as far as she can count, while constantly jumping.

Then there was: "Happy Holligan went to bed with some tin cans on his head. How many tin cans did he have? One, two, three, four …" The jumper continued as long as she could.

And perhaps you remember: "Salt, vinegar, mustard, cider, pepper …" Faster and faster went the jump rope until the jumper was exhausted—was it 200 times, or perhaps 300 jumps?

Being a kid can be lots of fun, especially when jumping rope and enjoying the chants. I certainly would like to go back, if only for a day, to this wonderful game of jumping rope. I feel certain that you would, too. ❖

Days of Fun

By Dorothy Kerberick

In a different place and long ago,
Little children ran and played,
Set up stores with rocks and weeds,
Colored sand in jars and lids.
Lines of brick outlined a playhouse;
No one dared to come in ours.
We sipped water tea from small tea sets,
While sitting on the violets.

Each one had a set of jacks,
Marbles in tobacco sacks.
The old witch across the lot
Kept the ball we hit too hard.

At dark, up in the cherry tree,
We ate the fruit, spit out the seeds;
Gathered in our yard at night,
Overhead the bright streetlight.

Ghost stories, tales of bats,
Kept our hair under a hat.
Jackknives tumbled in the grass;
If they stuck up straight, we laughed.
Crack the Whip … Run, Sheep, Run …
Yes, our days were filled with fun.
Friends made there I can t forget.
Sixty years, they re with me yet. ❖

Last Pitch

By Jean Powis

Three weeks into the summer vacation from grade school in the mid-1940s, my father suggested that we form two baseball teams and play against each other for the rest of the summer, with the champions becoming the proud holders of his homemade banner.

I was all for the idea; baseball was my first love. I watched the neighborhood boys play and I could give tips on how to bat, catch and slide. Whenever there was an argument over a play they d ask me for a decision because I knew the rules.

But there was one problem: When I was up to bat, I couldn t, as the saying goes, "hit the broad side of a barn."

Nobody had much money in those days, so as far as uniforms, we were a sorry-looking lot. Our shorts and tops looked more like the makings for a patchwork quilt than team look-alikes. Braids and ponytails took the place of baseball caps, and our footwear was a mishmash of worn-out "big brother sneakers" or old shoes that once had been used for dress-up.

Home plate was nothing more than a patch of dirt in the grass and bases usually ended up being pieces of cardboard. The boys let us borrow their bats and ball. We thought it was just because it gave them an excuse to watch us and laugh at the way we played.

We enjoyed our games and everyone played well—except me. I struck out so many times that the kids called me "Little Miss Strikeout."

But my friend Beverly was determined to make a ball player out of me. When no one was around she tried to teach me how to hit. Beverly was the other team s pitcher and she was good. I wouldn t even try to hit her fastball, but after lots of practice, I did manage to wallop her high pitch.

"If only I could do that in a game," I told Beverly. "I m sick of the kids making fun of me. I don t really want to play anymore."

The summer was over and our baseball teams were tied, each having won six games. My father decided he d ump our last game since it was to be the championship. Both teams wanted badly to win that last game of the summer and the champion s banner.

The other team scored the first runs on a homer with two on. *"Crrraaack!"* and the bat went flying in two directions. The girl who hit the homer was "well pounded," and I guess she just had too much power for that old bat. Luckily we had another.

The score was 3-0, but we weren t scared. We felt sure we d catch up. And in two more innings, we did. We screamed our lungs out over the 3-3 score.

The score was still 3-3 in the last inning. We were last up, with a runner on third and two outs. It figured that I would be the next to bat.

"Oh, no, Little Miss Strikeout is up!" my teammates moaned. "We ll lose for sure!"

Beverly threw her first pitch. "Outside, ball one!" the ump called.

The next two pitches whizzed by me so fast that they sounded like a swarm of bees. "Strike one! Strike two!" the ump yelled.

So there I was, a ball two strikes, and the whole team depending on me not to strike out. I looked at Beverly and tried to figure out what she was thinking. I hoped she remembered how I wanted to get just one hit, but I knew that she didn t want to let her team down.

Beverly wound up and hurled the ball toward me. It was a high one—and I smacked it. The girl on third came in home with the winning run. We were the champs!

After the game, I asked Beverly if she had meant to pitch a high one. "That s my secret," she whispered.

Years have gone by. I ve lost track of Beverly, but to this day I wonder: Did she deliberately toss me a high one, or did the pitch just go wild? ❖

Shinny on Your Own Side!

By Dale Denney

Football and basketball were big at our high school in the 1930s. Then there was shinny.

The best way to describe shinny is to take the rules of lacrosse, ice hockey, golf and baseball, put them all in a hat, and draw out what you need. Besides that, you could make up new rules each time you played.

It was fun. And it was outlawed after my brother got hurt.

We went to great lengths to find a good shinny club. We d take an ax and go out into the woods. We could make the best club from a young tree growing from the side of a steep slope. That s where the seedlings would push to the surface, then turn and grow straight up. Growing the way it did, the small tree would have a natural curve.

We scraped the loose dirt away and chopped out 6–10 inches of the primary root system. Then we trimmed the hook to fit our own specifications. Some shaped theirs to look like a hockey stick, some like a golf driver. My brother carved the root mass on his club into a crescent shape.

We d cut the shaft to fit individual preferences, too. Some would shave the bark on the upper end to make a more comfortable grip. But I always left the bark on because its rough texture gave me a better grip.

Hickory saplings made the best shinny clubs. They were pliant and strong, and the bark was relatively smooth. Oaks were good, too, and persimmon trees were all right. Willows were worthless.

It was like looking for a Christmas tree—we d spend all day trying to find the perfect one.

We took our shinny clubs to school and kept them in our lockers. It was against the rules, but a good shinny club was a prized possession. Part of the thrill of the game was smuggling our shinny clubs in and out of school without being caught.

Any number could play, from two to however many wanted to get in the game. That s why we liked playing at school—there d be maybe 20 or 30 on a side. Those who didn t happen to have a good club would use anything they could get their hands on—a broomstick, a short piece of pipe—and some would even get in the game by kicking the puck with their shoes.

We used a can for a puck. Condensed-milk cans made the best pucks because they were seldom opened on one end, just punctured. They would hold their shape longer than cans with one end missing.

The field of play was dictated by the topography. If we played in one of the many dirt roads around our town, the fencerows were out of bounds. If in a pasture—well, we had to have imaginary boundaries, or we d run ourselves to death.

At our school we had a perfect shinny field. It was between two buildings 50 feet apart,

> *We used a can for a puck. Condensed-milk cans made the best pucks because they were seldom opened on one end, just punctured.*

which was ideal since the buildings would keep the puck in play at all times. Our goals were an imaginary line between two oaks at one end and a sidewalk at the other.

We started each game by dropping the tin can in the center. Two opposing players faced off, positioning their clubs on either side of the can. Because my brother was so quick and had fashioned his club so expertly, he was always the face-off man on our side. He and his opponent would lift their clubs to touch one another above the can three times; everybody counted: "One, two three!" After the third touch, the face-off opponents would dig with their clubs for possession of the can.

Others could get into the face-off melee if they wanted. The face-off spot eventually became a small crater, sometimes growing a foot deep before cold weather put a stop to playing outdoors.

Each side tried to knock the can across the opponents goal line to score. If we tried driving it the distance like a golf ball, someone would use his club like a baseball bat and knock it back the other way. My brother was an expert at working the puck down the field as if he were playing hockey, passing it off, yanking it away when an opponent tried to drive it like a golf ball. He poked, passed, jabbed, flipped, hit and ran. With him on our side, we nearly always won.

Opponents swung and punched at the can constantly, trying to counter our every move. When the can got under our feet or behind us, the opponent had the right to yell, "Shinny on your own side!" and swing at the can with all his might. If we didn t jump high enough or were not able to block his club with our own, we got our shins busted but good.

But brawn wasn t always the prerequisite for winning. A small boy like my brother who was quick and had a light, strong hickory club could out-finesse his opponent almost every time. He was the star shinny player at our school.

Sometimes the action got so hectic that I didn t know who was on my side. The flip side of that was that I could join the side that had a good drive going and nobody would know the difference—or care, for that matter.

After one side scored, we d return the can to the face-off hole and start a new game.

We got tired and sweaty. Our clothes got dirty, our shoes scuffed. Our parents hated shinny because back then, you had to wear your best clothes to school, instead of your worst like today, not because of any rules, but because we never appeared in public—at school, church, the grocery store or the moving-picture show— without looking our best.

For school we wore starched, ironed shirts and creased pants—even pressed overalls, if that was all we had. Our shoes had to be shined and our hair cut and combed neatly. But we d be a mess after playing shinny during the noon hour.

School officials discouraged the game because of the danger. Sometimes the combined efforts of parents and teachers shut the game down for a few days, but it would break out again when a couple of guys started kicking a can. Then somebody would pick up a stick to hit the can to keep from getting his shoes scuffed. And before we knew it, there we d be with our clubs, yelling, beating at the can, fighting for control, leaping high to keep from getting our shins busted.

By the time the bell rang for classes, the tin can had been pounded into a hard metal ball with sharp, jagged edges. One day, somebody drove it like a golf ball and it hit my brother in the head, cutting an inch-long gash over one eyebrow. He was bleeding so badly that school officials rushed him to the doctor s office uptown. The doctor had to put five stitches in the cut to close it up. But the bandage was no bigger than a Band-Aid.

Since we had no telephone, school officials wrote a note of explanation to our parents and gave it to my brother to deliver. He tore it up. When he got home and Mom asked about the bandage, he told her he had been scratched playing touch football. He was afraid that if he told the truth, she would get the school to shut down the shinny game again.

But when the doctor came out to our house to take out the stitches, Mom found out what really had happened. She demanded that the school ban shinny, and they did—until the following spring. ❖

Fox & Geese

By Ken Tate

In *Good Old Days* and *Good Old Days Specials*, the magazines my wife and I edit, we have been asked many times about the old-time games of Fox and Geese.

I say games because there were two very popular games of Fox and Geese—one for outside and the other a board game played with checkers or other markers.

I enjoyed both as a boy and love to share my memories of the games.

Fox and Geese—Outside Game

This was a game characteristically played outside during winter. A large square or circle (see diagrams at below) were trodden out in the snow or marked on clear ice with skates.

The fox was stationed in the center, and the geese were scattered about in the play area. The geese were not allowed to leave the perimeter of the play area.

The object was for the fox to tag one of the geese, but he was not allowed to run on the circular lines. If the square field was used, the fox was allowed to run only along certain lines agreed upon between the players.

When one of the geese was tagged, he became the fox for the next round of the game.

Fox and Geese—Board Game

This game is played on a board with lines as pictured on the facing page. One player has 17 pieces called the geese (placed at the junction of lines marked by the small circles).

The fox has one game piece placed in the center of the diagram.

The game pieces, which can be checkers or colored pieces of paper, are moved along the lines from point to point.

The object is for the geese to pen up the fox so he cannot move, or for the fox to capture the geese. The fox may capture a goose by jumping over it, if the next space beyond is not occupied, as in the game of Checkers. The geese may advance and hem the fox in, endeavoring to keep each goose protected.

We spent untold hours playing these games as children on long winter days when school wasn t in session. ❖

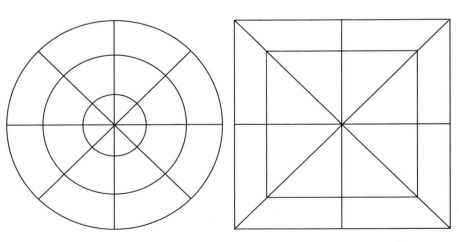

Outside Game Diagram

Fox & Geese Board Game

Copy diagram below for use in the Fox and Geese board game. If using checkers, the diagram should be enlarged to accommodate the larger game pieces. Coins, colored pieces of paper, etc. may be used for game pieces. Fox is in the center at the start of the game; geese are on the other spots marked.

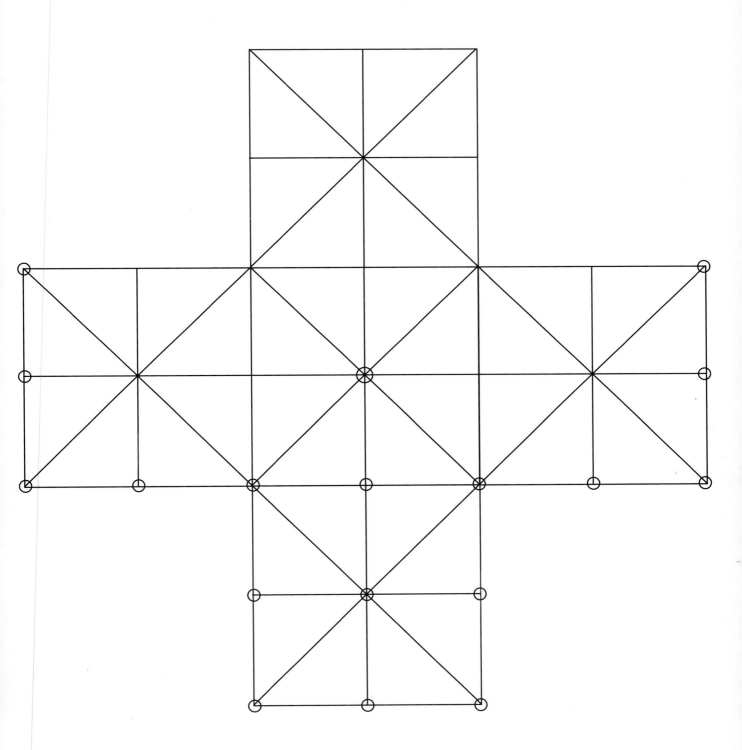

Lost All His Marbles by Henry Hintermeister © 1937 SEPS: Licensed by Curtis Publishing

Marbles

By R.D. Reif

*I*n 1944 everyone knew that spring was at hand without looking at the calendar. As soon as the snow melted on the south side of the schoolhouse and the ground dried off, the marble games began. It was cold for hands without mittens but that didn t matter; a boy could always warm them in his pockets while waiting for his turn to shoot.

The ring drawn on the bare ground varied in diameter according to the skill of the players. Second- and third-graders were satisfied with a relatively small ring, but experts in the sixth and seventh grades used rings up to four and five feet across.

There were two types of marbles. The economy kind were known as "dobies," drab clay balls a little larger than a good-sized pea. You could get a pocketful for six or seven cents. The other kind was known as "glassies." They were used mostly as shooters. Bright and colorful, they looked much like modern pictures of the earth taken from outer space. They were available in various sizes but the most popular had an axis of about a half-inch. You could get maybe two or three for a nickel.

Each player dropped the agreed-on number of dobies in the ring and the game began. Order of shooting was determined by who came closest in tossing their shooters at a line drawn on the ground. In a larger ring, a player often "babied up" to a dobie with his shooter in order to get close enough to knock it out of the circle. But in doing this, he was in danger of losing his shooter to another player. If his shooter was still in the ring when his turn came again, he could often knock a dobie out of the circle. He was then entitled to another shot. He could keep on shooting as long as he drove dobies or other shooters out of the ring. If the game was for "keeps," he could keep all the marbles he knocked out of the circle.

All sorts of situations came up. If there was an obstruction (a twig, grass root or pebble) between his shooter and the target, he could take "knucks up" (hold his shooter slightly elevated) or "ebbs" (move it around the object) or "clarence" (clear away the obstruction) or "picks" (pick up the target dobie and move it to a better spot, but not closer to his shooter or to the edge of the ring) or "sets" (set the target on a slight mound) or "levels" (level the ground over which he intended to drive the target). However, if an opponent called "no picks" or "ven ebbs," etc., before the shooter called his intention, he was not allowed these privileges. The game continued until all the marbles were shot from the ring.

Marble playing, like other skills, improved with practice and experience. To shoot, the marble was held between the thumb knuckle and forefinger. The shooter marble was propelled toward the target by snapping the thumb forward. Shooting took considerable practice. Some players could send a marble with force and accuracy for four or five feet.

Every game developed tense situations and then his opponents would shout at the shooter. "Knocks down, ven ebbs, no clarence, no picks, no sets, no levels, screw bony tight!" That meant the shooter had to keep his knuckles on the ground; he could not move his shooter to a better position; he could not clear away an obstacle; he could not move the target, place it on a mound or level the ground—and he had to shoot hard; he could not "baby up."

The game did involve a deep moral problem. A kid either played for keeps or he did not. His decision usually depended on his parents. If he played for keeps against his parents wishes, his pile of marbles would increase and there would have to be an explanation. If he was a loser and lost his supply, he would have to approach Dad for money or quit playing.

But the kid who had permission to play for keeps also had problems. Sometimes his pockets would become overloaded and accidentally spill on the floor during school hours. The whole room would be disturbed by the loud clatter, and then—heck to pay! I know—it happened to me! ❖

Fun on a Shoestring

Chapter Three

The dictionary includes one definition of "on a shoestring" as: "with only a small amount of capital or resources." Whenever I think about how we made our own fun back in the Good Old Days, I remember particularly how we were able to create entertainment from almost nothing. We truly had very little capital, but I think we had a lot of resources—mental if not monetary. Our old tire swing is one case in point.

A worn tire was a valuable commodity around our place. After the last mile was squeezed from it on our old Chevrolet coupe, it was never relegated to throw-away status until we had satisfied the old adage of the Depression era: "Use it up, wear it out. Make it do, or do without."

Grandma Stamps got first dibs on the tire. If she needed it, it was split in half down the middle of the worn out tread, making two doughnuts with a trough on each of the two rings. With these, Grandma had two watering troughs, one for her chicks in the brooder house and the second for her hens in the barn lot.

When Grandma didn't need the old tire, we kids were next in line. After rolling it up and down hills—sometimes with one of us wedged in the middle—we took our tire to its final resting place beneath a huge branch on one of the many towering oak trees around the house,

There we shinnied up the tree and tied one end of a large piece of hemp rope, begged from Daddy, on the branch. The other end was passed through the tire, and it was hoisted up to a good swinging height while one of us hastily tied it off. The knot above the tire made a great hand-hold for swinging.

Now we had all the freedom of flight afforded to every kid on a swing, regardless of price. There was no fancy playground set with slide and monkey bars, but our trusty oak provided plenty of climbing for us little monkeys, and we could always slide down the rope to our new tire swing.

When "on a shoestring" means "on an old rope," there is plenty of fine-tuning needed. The rope might stretch or the limb might bow a bit more than we thought it would, and we might have to retie the rope, adjusting the tire higher. There was always the chance that a knot might give way or our old piece of rope might snap, giving us a midair tumble. But that was just part of the excitement.

Countless hours on the tire swing provided adventure and recreation without a dime of direct expense. No, we didn't have much capital, but we had a lot of resources. You just had to know how to make you own fun on a shoestring.

—*Ken Tate*

© *Joy Ride* by John Sloane

Hay Ride

By Helen Colwell Oakley

As the last load of hay was stacked up in the mow of our big red barn in R.D. 1, Binghamton, N.Y., in the late summer of 1938, my brothers, sisters and I teased Mom and Dad Murphy to give us permission to have a hayride at the farm. We finally got their OK. I was 13 and my sisters and brothers were all younger.

We prayed for good weather as we sent out invitations to our city cousins, friends and neighbors. The big event was met with much enthusiasm from the kids as well as the grown-ups. The hired men seemed anxious to come and help scatter the loose hay on the rigging. One offered to drive the team. Every little detail was planned for the big event.

We had loads of help. Mom helped with the menu. The hired girl promised to make cookies and lemonade to go along with the cases of bottled orange drink and chocolate milk from our creamery. The aunts would make cakes, and a neighbor lady volunteered to have coffee ready when we returned from the hayride.

There was a thunderstorm the night before our hayride was scheduled, and we were plenty upset as we went to bed. We didn't want anything to spoil our plans. Mom tried to assure us that the rain would stop and it would be clear by the next morning. I guess she knew best, as the day was perfect for a hayride. The sun came out and the forecast on the radio predicted a beautiful, sunny day. Our hayride was on!

That morning we helped Mom tidy up the house and the lawns. We were going to have a bonfire in the backyard to roast hot dogs, toast marshmallows and sit around when we ate. We carried the picnic table alongside the spot for the bonfire. With that done, we thought we had all the preparations under control, but Mom said that we had to help carry forkfuls of hay to the wagon, as the hired men wouldn't have time. It took more hay than we ever dreamed it would. My brothers spread the hay evenly on the wagon, calling for more every time we tossed some out of the mow.

Finally, when our arms were about ready to give out, they hollered that we had enough. By this time, the wagon was quite full and looked like a load coming in from the field. But the boys tossed and turned on it and said that it was just right for our hayride.

We ate our supper in a hurry and lost no time getting upstairs to get ready for the big event at 8 o'clock. Before we were half-dressed, we heard a car driving in—some of the city cousins were here already! My sisters and I didn't have jeans and pants, such as girls wear today. We had borrowed some from Dad and then had to turn them up and put a belt on to try to hold them up. They were much too big, of course, but Mom said that the hay would be prickly and that we needed to wear something heavy to protect our legs.

We had pajamas on underneath, to wear once the overalls were removed. Our pajamas were adorable, with large flowers splashed all over, wide shoulder straps and large floppy legs. There was also a hat with a wide brim to match. The pajamas were the latest fad, and quite daring. We wore high-top sneakers, too, as low tennis sneakers weren't "in" yet.

On the hayride, the ladies looked kind of funny. Each was wearing a pair of her husband's pants under a housedress. Women didn't wear pants and slacks then, so a woman dressed in pants created quite a stir.

"There's as beautiful a moon as you'll ever feast your eyes upon, coming over yonder mountain," said the hired man when he came to the house. He was rarin' to go on the hayride.

That morning we helped Mom tidy up the house and the lawns. We were going to have a bonfire in the backyard to roast hot dogs, toast marshmallows and sit around when we ate.

"As soon as you're all hitched up, we'll be there," we all chorused. Mom and the aunts insisted that we take horse blankets, as a storm could blow up, or we might get chilly as night came on. They always seemed to expect the worst. One of their favorite mottoes was "Better to be prepared than sorry later."

As we climbed onto the wagon, it was funny to watch the ladies try to get up on the load of hay. The big boys would lay down flat on the load, reach down for the lady's hands, and then some of the menfolk would try to boost her up onto the wagon. How the ladies giggled! It was fun having several grownups along, and they didn't seem to mind one bit when the hired girl did a little smooching with the hired man as he sat up front and drove the team.

The grown-ups told stories about the stars, the moon and hayrides of long ago. We enjoyed their tales and asked a heap of questions. The moon was orange as it crept up over the mountain and it was so bright that you could see all over the countryside, almost as plain as day.

We drove on dirt roads mostly, so we didn't see but a few cars. One of the big boys sat up front with the driver to watch for cars, and when he saw one, he flashed a flashlight around in circles so that they would be able to see us. The horses could see the path just fine in the moonlight.

Sometimes the horses trotted a little. "Make them trot all the time!" we begged. "It's more fun to go fast."

"Not good for the horses," said the hired man. "Not good at all to make them run all the way, 'cause they've had a hard day in the field. So it's best if we let them take it a little easy most of the way." And with that he pulled on the reins to slow the team to a steady pace.

As we rested our heads back on the hay, we could almost touch the galaxy of stars. The full moon was pure enchantment as we rode along and listened to a couple of the fellows harmonizing to the accompaniment of a harmonica.

They sang *When the Moon Comes Over the Mountain, South of the Border, Springtime In the Rockies, When I Grow Too Old To Dream* and *Let Me Call You Sweetheart.*

Sometimes we had to duck to miss low-hanging branches. Whenever we went by a farmhouse, the family was usually out front or on the porch to wave or call out "Hello!" One of the families said that their kids could join us for the remainder of the ride, and that they would come pick them up after our refreshments. A hayride is hard to resist—especially one in progress—and we were happy to have more riders.

When we neared the top of the last hill toward home, we could see the pole light by the barn, and in the back yard, our bonfire was burning brightly. Mom, Dad and some of the grownups had stayed home to take care of the small children, keep the fire going so that there would be a nice bed of coals to roast hot dogs, lay out the food, and get in some visiting before the rush. They must have seen us coming because they had everything ready when we jumped down off the hay rigging and hurried to the bonfire.

There were hot dogs attached to sticks, all ready to roast over the fire. I liked mine slightly burned, then stuck in a roll with ketchup and slices of onion—that was eating! The marshmallows were good and sticky. We had cakes and cookies, and we could have all we wanted because there was plenty and it was a party, Mom said. After several hot dogs, it wasn't easy to do justice to all the treats, though.

We sat around the fire for a while after refreshments. The fire felt good as the night air was becoming damp and cool. We could see a mist forming over the woodland beyond the barn, and the cars parked under the pole light were wet, as though there had been a light rain or mist.

The aunts gathered the cousins together. Some of the little ones had fallen asleep on Mom's day bed and one was fast asleep in a rocker with his head hanging over one side. They were all set to head for home when the hired man came in with a fiddle and suggested that we finish off the evening with a good old-fashioned square or two. The cousins, who were around our age, all begged to stay and watch the square dancing. Four couples lined up in a circle and joined hands. Then the hired man told Mom that the dining-room table should be moved over from the center of the dining room to one corner and then we could dance on the linoleum. He began to stomp one foot, play the fiddle, and holler out the calls.

It was a riot, watching from the sidelines, as we all sat around in a circle to watch and keep time with the music. The dancers got mixed up and ended up with different partners one time. I danced one square with one of the neighbor's hired men, and he said, "You're like pulling a bobsled through the mud. Now loosen up a little, will ya?" He said I did better toward the end. That was one of the first times that I ever attempted square dancing, and at that time, I still enjoyed it best from the sidelines.

By midnight everyone was beginning to yawn. So the aunts gathered the cousins and we all went out to the cars to say good night. We all agreed that it had been one of the best hayrides ever! ❖

Game of Horseshoes by J.F. Kernan © 1924 SEPS: Licensed by Curtis Publishing

Pitching Horseshoes

By Virginia Hearn Machir

All through the Good Old Days in rural areas of Missouri, you could hear the clang of ringers and the clink of leaners coming from the back yard, or from out behind the barn. There was seldom a family reunion or other get-together that the men and boys didn't organize a horseshoe-pitching game. In those days they played with real horseshoes, discarded from the hooves of horses, not the standard items available at the hardware store today that are meant only for throwing.

At our family reunions, slow-talking, overall-clad Uncle Mack was champion horseshoe pitcher; some claimed he could throw ringers about three-fourths of the time. All the menfolk liked to have Uncle Mack as their partner.

There were good-natured arguments among players concerning the rules. According to our rules, a ringer would give a player three points and a leaner, one point. Otherwise, the shoe closest to the peg got a point, provided it was not more than six inches away. Therein was the cause of arguments. Sometimes a ruler was necessary to settle the question. The first player or team to total 50 points was the winner.

Uncle Mack thought the best stakes for horseshoe pitching were old railroad spikes driven firmly into the ground 40 feet apart. He favored a shoe that wasn't worn too thin, as he claimed the lighter ones didn't carry the distance as well.

The men found pitching horseshoes was good companionship and good exercise, and the match usually ended with a good, cold drink of well water from the dipper hanging on the pump.

While the men were pitching horseshoes, the women, having finished the dishes, congregated around the kitchen table where they cooled themselves with pasteboard fans donated by the local undertaker. The topic of horseshoes just naturally came up in the conversation. Cousin Mattie believed that horseshoes brought good luck and said that she had one tacked up over her kitchen door.

This brought on a discussion over the manner of hanging a horseshoe to insure the best fortune. Aunt Bertha thought the open end should point downward; Cousin Mattie argued that the open end should be up to prevent the luck from running out. Then there were some who believed that hanging it up in a horizontal position was best.

Aunt Bertha said she had read where some man hung a horseshoe over his door and it didn't bring him good luck at all. It fell down and cut a gash in the top of his head that took five stitches to close. "I guess your luck depends not so much on how you hang the horseshoe as on how *well* you hang it," Aunt Bertha said.

Just the other day I read that a company in Worcester, Mass., sells $500,000 worth of horseshoes every year—shoes meant for throwing and not for shoeing. It seems horseshoe pitching is still in vogue.

So, if you decide to take up the sport of horseshoe pitching, the shoes are still available. But if you decide to hang one over your door for luck, hang it well! ❖

> *At our family reunions, slow-talking, overall-clad Uncle Mack was champion horseshoe pitcher; some claimed he could throw ringers about three-fourths of the time. All the menfolk liked to have Uncle Mack as their partner.*

Saturday Night Dance

By Dorothy Carter Steiner

A gloomy, wintry night would soon turn into a time of joyful entertainment for the entire community when we heard the violin being tuned and the mandolin plunking an answer to it. It was another wonderful Saturday night dance.

Sixty-some years ago, we climbed the schoolhouse steps in the dark, my parents, sister and I. The young and the old in the neighborhood attended, and most arrived early so as not to miss the first dance. Everyone had hurried through their farm chores and eaten an early supper in order to get ready.

Men got haircuts and polished their shoes. They wore their suits, if they had them, or clean overalls. Some wore high-top work boots, and they had just as good a time as anyone, although they probably did not inspire as much romance among the ladies, who sometimes declined to dance with them for fear of having their toes stepped on by those big, hard boots.

Children wore their best clothes and were careful not to muss them. They were as excited as anyone at the prospect of a party and a chance to see their friends.

Ladies wore their "good dresses" and took a lot of care to make themselves presentable, curling their hair with curling irons heated over a kerosene lamp. They pressed their clothes and, if they were lucky enough to own a bottle of Evening in Paris perfume, dabbed a little behind their ears. These were hard times, and few women possessed make-up. Their only jewelry was a string of glass beads. When the teacher's girlfriend came one time with rouge on her cheeks and her ears adorned with earrings, we children thought she must be rich. She lived in town.

On a Friday during school, someone would tell the teacher of the plans for the Saturday night dance, so everything had to be put away, desks cleared and the blackboard washed. Before the children were dismissed the desks were shoved up against the walls to make room for dancing, and the teacher was forewarned that the schoolroom might not be so tidy come Monday morning.

On wintry Saturday evenings, someone always went to the schoolhouse early to build a fire and light the gas lanterns. Sometimes the driveway had to be shoveled out, too. Cornmeal was then scattered around the floor as a dance wax.

Then the families arrived, stamping the snow off their feet in the vestibule. The desks were piled high with coats and caps, and overshoes were tucked underneath on the floor.

The faithful musicians were always there early. Howard perched on the pedestal organ stool, tuning his mandolin or guitar, as Hilding rubbed rosin along his bow, then tucked the violin under his chin and began tapping his foot.

The lively music started with someone producing a pair of rattle bones to beat time. They played waltzes, schottisches and circle two-steps. Young girls danced together, but a lady had to wait for a man to ask her to dance, although it was proper for another man to cut in and finish the dance with her. People sat around the edge of the room and visited between dances. Unmarried girls hoped a certain someone would ask them to dance and sometimes had an older brother nudge their desired partner. Sometimes a daddy danced with a child in his arms, much to the child's delight.

The desks jiggled and the floor rose and fell under the stamping feet. Dancers mopped their faces with handkerchiefs and fanned themselves after an especially fast number. As the evening wore, the tiny folks got tired and went to sleep on the pile of coats while their parents danced all evening.

Some men were bashful. There was always a cluster of them peeking out from the boys' cloakroom. One man always had a supply of Yucatan chewing gum, which he shared with the children. Other men stood around joshing each other and urging their friends to ask a lady to dance as they nervously rolled cigarettes and smoked them, ashing them in the cuffs of their trousers.

Little mishaps took place: A lady would break a heel on her high-heeled slipper, and that would spoil the rest of her evening. In the winter the floor was too cold for dancing without shoes, and who would want to make holes in precious stockings! Or in the middle of a dance, a guitar or violin string would break. That meant an intermission while the instrument was restrung and tuned again. This provided an opportunity to rest and visit friends.

If the room got too warm from the big stove, the doors were opened for a few moments. On below-zero nights, men went outside and started their cars once in a while so that they wouldn't be stalled when it came time to go home.

Around midnight, the warm aroma of coffee drifted out over the dance floor from the back room. Every family brought cake squares or sandwiches filled with cheese, eggs or potted meat. The youngsters drank nectar. The coffee was poured into big tin cups. One empty cup was set aside for an offering to pay for the coffee and paper plates. A few precious pennies rattled into the cup.

After dining on these refreshments there was more music and dancing. Some man would pass his hat around to all the other men to collect nickels and dimes and hopefully some quarters to pay the musicians. They usually collected about $3.

Then, in a little while, they announced the last dance. The tune was always *Home, Sweet Home,* and it was an unwritten rule that husbands always danced with their wives for the last number.

For a few hours, they had been able to forget the everyday problems and just enjoy each other. Everybody danced with everybody else, and a lot of romances began in someone's embrace on those exciting nights at the Leech Lake School in the years before World War II.

Tired, happy dancers picked sleeping children up off the coats, then sorted through the wraps until they found their own. They bundled up the children and everyone headed for their cars, refreshed for the beginning of another week of trying to make a living when jobs were nearly nonexistent and groceries were bought on credit at the corner store. ❖

Gone Fishin'

By Dorothy Bolding Cox

Spring is a time of rebirth, a time to say, "Let's go fishing." Those words had the ring of magic when I was a little girl. Even now, more than a half-century later, a stir of excitement surges through me when I hear them, and I have a nostalgic flashback to bygone days, when my brother, Floyd, spoke those words to me.

We first began to fish together in the early 1920s. The fact that I was a little snub-nosed girl who wore overalls and homemade shirts and was 10 years younger than he was made no difference to Floyd. He wanted a fishing buddy when spring came, and I was ready to tag along behind his overall-clad legs as we walked to the river. I looked up often at his straw-hat–shaded face and saw that it was naked with joy. I guess every little girl looks up to her big brother. I know I did, and the fact that he took me fishing made me his slave forever. He was a special kind of big brother—gentle, generous, great of heart.

The Colorado River, with its cliffs and bouldered edges, meandered through our West Texas sandy-land farm in southwest Scurry County, and afforded us ample water for wetting a hook. We had one particular place we liked to fish where the river made a sharp curve at the base of a massive rock bluff that hovered over the deep, dark water. Fish were apt to bite there when they wouldn't any other place. There was barely room to sit and fish between the water and the bluff, and the ground was worn bare except for a lone willow tree that not only provided a bit

Fishing Buddies by Mark Keathley © Copyright Newmark USA 2000

of shade, but fishing poles as well.

Floyd would cut long, slender limbs with his pocketknife, strip off the bark, and cut a groove around the little end where he fastened the fishing line so it wouldn't slip off. We always left our poles lying on the bank for next time, but many times when the river got out of its banks after a heavy rain, they washed away. Then Floyd cut us more.

Sometimes when we were fishing, huge raindrops caught us unaware. Falling straight down, they pocked the smooth surface of the water and wet us through and through. But if the fish were hitting, we'd huddle under the verdant canopy of the willow tree and fish away.

Eventually the rain would stop and frogs would come up from the mud and turtles would park themselves on their logs, and we'd see a ghost of a rainbow in the east. We'd look at one another and smile; there was no need for words to express our happiness. We loved the feel of the country all around, the sounds of nature, and the smell of spring.

We were not the type of fishermen who fished only for lunker bass; we were just as proud of a sunfish or a 6-inch yellow catfish, and seldom threw one back, no matter what its size. We went home with various sizes of fish, which we dressed ourselves. Mama fried them to a rich, golden brown for supper.

We had no sophisticated fishing equipment. Our tackle boxes were Prince Albert tobacco cans carried in our hip pockets. We filled them with various sizes of rusty hooks, bits of split-shot babbitt for sinkers, and a ball of twine

raveled from flour sacks, which we braided and used for line.

For floats we used corks from household bottles, like the ones bluing and turpentine came in. Besides suspending our hooks at the desired depth, the floats also gave us something on which to concentrate, and provided us with a quick thrill when a hungry fish took the bait and pulled the cork under. At the slightest bite we were ready to set the hook with a quick jerk. Even a nibble, which would cause the cork to move slightly, provided a thrill I've never forgotten.

Our standard bait was earthworms, which we dug from under the edge of the barn or around the stock tank where the ground was damp. I was a little squeamish about threading the worms on my hook, and I could hardly stand the feel of them when they stretched themselves to great lengths. Sometimes I could talk Floyd into baiting my hook and sometimes I couldn't. But the perch went for the worms in a big way, and we brought up all sizes. They were easy to clean and good eating.

Sometimes we fished with redhorse minnows, which we caught in a long, cone-shaped trap Floyd made out of an old piece of screen and stiff baling wire. We baited it with a cold biscuit left from breakfast, attached a long piece of binder twine to it, and then threw it out into shallow water, where the minnows were. They swam like mad from all directions to devour the biscuit. They weren't very smart; they could find their way into the trap, but they couldn't find their way out.

When we had caught several, we pulled the trap in and poured the minnows into our minnow

Iris Weddell White

bucket—a gallon syrup pail with holes punched in the lid. We lowered the bucket into the river on a string to keep the minnows alive in the fresh water.

Sometimes, after a head rise, we waded out through the soft, boggy mud that squished between our toes to puddles where unfortunate minnows were trapped and we tried to catch them barehanded. But they were hasty little fellows and could slip through our fingers before we could make a fist.

I didn't mind touching the minnows like I did the worms, and even though I thought they were too pretty, with their red and orange fins and shiny silver scales, to meet such a fate, I didn't mind baiting my hook with them.

When we fished on the bottom for catfish, our bait was leftover bread mixed with a little bit of syrup for consistency and rolled into a tight ball. I hated to catch a catfish, however. I was scared to death of them and still am. There is nothing that hurts worse than being finned by a catfish. They are ugly, too, with soft whiskers called "barbels" around their mouths, which they use for feelers, and they have soft, slimy skin instead of scales.

Floyd took catfish off my hook, but any other kind, I took off. I strung them on a stringer made of twine with a small stick tied to one end; I ran the stringer through their gills and used the stick to stake the line at the edge of the water until we got ready to go. Then we wetted a tow sack and carried them home in it. We seldom lost a fish.

Occasionally we ran down grasshoppers and used them for bait. It was a lot of fun catching them, and sometimes their jiggling on the water's surface caused enough commotion to entice a fish to bite. But we didn't have as much luck with them as we did with worms and minnows.

We nearly always set out bank hooks before we went home. Next morning, we came down to see what we'd caught. One morning when we came down, my cork was going crazy.

There is nothing that hurts worse than being finned by a catfish. They are ugly, too, with soft whiskers called "barbels" around their mouths.

"I've got a whopper!" I hollered—but when I pulled my line up, my excitement vanished and fear took over. I screamed, dropped my line and ran clear to the top of the rock bluff.

"Aw, come on back!" Floyd said, laughing. "It's just an eel."

"It's not either! It's a snake!" I screamed.

An eel is another ugly fish, with smooth, slimy skin and no pelvic fins on its long, writhing body. Just the sight of him squirming at the end of my line scared me half to death. That was the only eel I ever caught—and I hope it was my last. Needless to say, Floyd had to take him off my hook. I realize now that he was less dangerous than a fish with fins, but I wasn't about to touch him.

"Let's take the eel home and get Mama to fry him," Floyd teased.

I looked at him in horror. *Eat an eel? Never!* We didn't take the eel home, even though they are edible.

When the river was up and booming, heavy with a torrent of debris, Floyd and I sometimes fished with hand lines off the rock bluff. But the water was much too swift to catch anything. Still, it was fun to sit and watch the muddy, foaming water rush by. Sometimes lumber from a washed-out bridge upstream came sailing by, and we'd wish we could jump on it and go sailing down the river. We had visions, too, of fish being washed downstream to replenish our old fishing hole—great fish, larger than we had ever caught before.

I'm glad that I grew up on the Colorado River, and that I had a big brother who often said to me, "Let's go fishing!" He helped make my childhood happy, and he helped instill in me the enjoyment of fishing.

In later years, he and I fished from fancy boats in man-made lakes, using the latest fishing equipment and store-bought bait. But I doubt that either of us enjoyed it as much as we did when we sat on the riverbank and fished with bait we'd caught ourselves, using poles cut from the old willow tree. ❖

Penny Bingo

By Liz Smith

P laying bingo for pennies after a sumptuous Sunday dinner or holiday meal was the highlight of any family get-together, at least for me, at Grandma's house those many years ago. Upon reflection, it seems that the possibility of winning a few pennies from an adult relative held more fascination than the thought of my grandmother's fantastic cooking!

If it wasn't penny bingo, it was pinochle, though bingo was by far my favorite. At the age of 9, I did play a pretty good game of pinochle, but it's been a good many years since I looked at a deck of cards, or for that matter, even a bingo card. I never developed a taste for "real" gambling, and in fact, neither did anyone else in the family. But we sure had a lot of fun together.

Actually, we called my grandmother "Nana" and my grandfather "Nanoo." Both were Italian immigrants, though Nana had been so young when her parents brought her to the states that she bore no trace of an Italian accent. Nanoo, on the other hand, had been older when he arrived and he wore a fascinating accent that charmed me. I still think of Nanoo today when I hear anyone speak "broken English."

I'm not certain how the games got started, but I don't doubt but what they had a lot to do with the fact that after consuming one of Nana's repasts, there was little energy left for anything but sitting around the big round oak table, challenging our ability to concentrate just a little. The more daring would play three or four bingo cards at a time. And I was daring!

To say that Nana fed her company—family or friends—well is an understatement! No Sunday or holiday meal was "proper" unless it began with her delicious Italian soup, which was called "pasta brotho." It was made from chicken broth, chunks of celery, carrots, onions and tomatoes, and tubetinni pasta, and was topped with freshly grated Romano cheese. We still use the recipe, but today it *is* the meal when accompanied by a salad. But not then; then it was just the first course, accompanied by thick slabs of the best homemade bread you could ever want—and real butter!

This soup course was inevitably followed by spaghetti and meatballs, with sauce that Nana made from scratch and simmered on the back of her big old wood and gas stove for two days. After that came the *pièce de résistance*, which was different depending on the holiday, or whether it was a Sunday.

Sundays were my favorite, perhaps because there were more people getting together, or perhaps because chicken was a Sunday staple. Nana and Nanoo raised their own chickens, and they were the most succulent I've ever eaten. Nana was as fussy about feeding them as she was about feeding us. And she'd fry that chicken light and crispy on the outside and so juicy on the inside that Colonel Sanders and Kentucky Fried Chicken probably would have turned green with envy! With the chicken came real mashed potatoes, a seasonal vegetable from Nanoo's garden, and homemade pie. Adults were also treated to Nanoo's homemade wine, in moderation. We youngsters occasionally swiped sips when the adults weren't looking.

After all that eating, which in itself took a long time because there was much rapport at the table, is it any wonder that the remaining time was devoted to relaxing but exciting games?

My brother and I could hardly wait for the "draw" for caller, and we would sometimes fight over who would get to draw first. Calling the bingo numbers was an honor, and whichever of us got to call first felt pretty important.

I well remember the time I was 9 or 10 and Vaughn Monroe was coming to our southwestern New York community to appear in person at Shea's Theater. Vaughn Monroe was my very favorite back then and I wanted in the worst way to see him in person. I had never seen any "star" in person before. But the way finances were in those days, we had to earn our spending money—at least anything as extravagant as 65 cents for the theater! So this particular Sunday, with only 10 cents to my name, I decided to console myself with an afternoon of penny bingo. But when the afternoon had passed, to my elation, I had won 55 cents more than I had started with!

I have seen my share of stars in person since that day so many years ago, but I have never looked forward to any performance with the excitement I felt then. Nor have I watched any performer with the awe I felt when I heard Vaughn Monroe sing *Ghost Riders in the Sky* in person! To this day, when "old" tunes are played on the radio and I hear *Riders,* I pause, and I remember dinners at Nana's and those penny bingo games.

The advent of television took its toll on the family games. Of course, we were older by then, but the challenge of a game still held great appeal for me. It still does, in fact. Given a choice, I'd much rather play a game than watch television, not that there's much time these days for either. Nor much family around, for that matter.

At first, when television was a big thing, Nana and Nanoo held out, but when the screens got a little bigger and reception got a little better, the first black-and-white set in the family came into their home. Although a few of us die-hards tried to hang on to our tradition while others were glued to the set, the tube won out and penny bingo became a thing of the past.

I'm a grandma now myself, but my grandchildren are scattered around the country. My children never learned about penny bingo. Nanoo died when they were quite small and we were living in California. A couple of years later, when we were visiting her, Nana died in my arms. When we were going through her things afterward, I came across the old, shabby bingo cards and chipped wooden numbers. The markers had all disappeared when the game was still active; we had used popcorn kernels.

Today I'm sorry I didn't save at least one of those old cards and a few numbers. I think my grandchildren might find them interesting when they come to visit and I try to tell them how much fun games can be. No, I won't be teaching them penny bingo in this day and age, but I will teach them about family games. They are so good for relationships—and memories! ❖

School Picnic

By Florice Allen Walker

I remember a school picnic we held back in the Good Old Days. It was a seventh- and eighth-grade picnic. Our teacher was Miss Hannah Scott, and we had so much fun that day!

The morning of our picnic, we met at the schoolhouse. After everyone had arrived, we gathered up all of our food, fishing poles and whatever else we had to take and headed out. We had two cases of soda pop that the boys carried. They tried to drink some along the way, but the teacher wouldn't let them because the drinks were to go with our lunch.

We hiked a little more than a mile outside of town to a place we called "the Bluffs." We were having our picnic along the banks of the Little Blue River, which flows along the outskirts of our small hometown of Oak, in the southeastern corner of Nebraska.

I had borrowed a short cane fishing pole from Dad. Nora Mercier, Gwen Beavers, Pansy Erickson, Mary Simic and I all planned to fish. The first thing we did was bait our lines and throw them out into the river. Then we decided to take a walk and pick some daisies, so we stuck the ends of our fishing poles in the riverbank. We would check later to see if we had caught any fish.

The boys had taken off to climb the bluffs, so we girls went in the opposite direction to find our flowers. Miss Scott and Vincent Sadler told us that they would stay and guard our food and soda pop.

The boys were back already by the time we girls returned. They started giving us a hard time about being late because they were hungry and Miss Scott would not let them eat until we were all there.

It was about this time that someone hollered at us to check our fishing poles because it looked like we had all caught a fish. We all ran down to the riverbank. When we lifted our poles up, we found that each one had a big bullsnake at the end of the line. I was scared stiff of snakes so I started screaming and dropped my pole into the water. Then I remembered that it was my dad's fishing pole, and he would kill me if I didn't get it back home to him.

Henry Meyer was kind of "sweet on me" so he said he would get it for me. Well, he tried to reach it by lying down flat on the bank, but he slipped and fell into the river. The other boys helped him get out. One of them grabbed my pole, so I got it back, but poor Henry was soaking wet. He and the rest of the boys went back up the hill so he could dry his clothes.

I don't suppose many people remember that boys' underwear was made all in one piece back then, and it was called "BVDs." My sister Opal and I always laughed and giggled when we saw pictures of BVDs in the Sears Roebuck catalog.

Anyway, Henry's mother had made him some BVDs out of flour sacks. His folks owned the Oak Flour Mill, so flour sacks were plentiful. When the boys held them up to dry in the wind, we could see "1888"—the name of a brand of flour—printed on the back of them. We all laughed and giggled and called Henry "1888" for the rest of the day. But I am sure that if the rest of us had admitted it, we would have discovered that all of our bloomers and undershirts were made out of flour sacks.

Our lunch was all set out and ready by the time the wind and sun had dried Henry's clothes and the boys had come back down the hill. We each had a bottle of pop to go along with our lunch.

After we had eaten, we played a few games. Then we gathered up our stuff and headed for home. We were a very tired bunch of kids, and our beautiful daisies had wilted, but we thought it had been the best day of our lives.

I don't suppose kids nowadays would enjoy a picnic like the one we had on that long-ago day. Memories of our special picnic still make me laugh. So many years have passed since that beautiful day. I wish that I knew where all of my school friends were now. ❖

Remembering The Box Supper

By Nellie Jones

Dollah, dollah, dollah, dollah, who'll make it two? Two dollah, two, two, two, two dollah, who'll gimme three?

"Now, gentlemen, you know it's worth more than two dollars to share this delicious supper with the gorgeous young lady who prepared it. Why, I'll bet there's a chocolate meringue pie in here.

"Come on, let's make it three, three, three. Going at two-fifty. Going … going … *sold* to the gentleman in the back row!"

Remember the "box supper" or "pie supper," that important social event of the fall season in rural schools?

Girls of all ages brought decorated boxes lavished with

1938 Nucoa Butter ad, House of White Birches nostalgia archives

crepe-paper ribbons and bows. They filled them with sandwiches, pickles and other homemade goodies, including a pie for dessert. Men and boys bid on each box and the winner shared the meal with the girl who'd brought it.

Every community had one—a gorgeous young thing who was everyone's sweetheart. When her box was hoisted high, every bachelor in the audience (and some of the married men) joined the bidding. All the losers envied the guy who got that box. The men also thought it great sport to bid against a fellow who had a "steady sweetie" to run the price up—especially if the "sweetie" happened to be the teacher.

A married man usually bought his wife's supper but sometimes bid on others, all in the spirit of good fun.

The money raised went to the school to pay for special needs, so folks usually spent generously. Sometimes one man would buy several suppers if the bidding lagged.

As with many competitions, there was a downside. Though the auctioneer didn't identify the owners of the boxes, word got around. Most folks knew whose box was up for bid. If your box didn't attract many bidders or bring much money, it was embarrassing. If no one bid, that was really devastating. A father often came to the rescue and bought his daughter's supper if bidding was slow.

When I was a timid second-grader, a young man I'd never met bought my box. I didn't want to eat with him, but my parents made me.

He must have been as shy as I was, for he made no effort to make conversation. So, in embarrassed silence, I choked down a few bites of my ham sandwich, sweet pickles and chocolate pie. Some classmates teased me and this only increased my frustration.

After this traumatic experience I always extracted a promise from Dad to buy my box quickly. I didn't want to be humiliated if no one bid on it. And I *certainly* didn't want to repeat the unpleasant experience of sharing it with anyone of the opposite sex, particularly a stranger!

By the time I was 11 years old, I was growing out of my shyness. The teacher's boyfriend bought my box that year—as well as hers, of course. And he shared both suppers. I felt like a queen, and I never again asked Dad to buy my box. ❖

Pastimes Of Yesteryear

By Myra A. Peabody

*D*o today's young people ever wonder what Mother and Grandma did in those early days before television was invented? How did they entertain themselves during their younger days?

Well, to begin with, Grandma and Mother visited more. If the next-door neighbors didn't come to visit after supper, they would probably go visit the neighbor.

And if they didn't feel like another visit, there were always jigsaw puzzles. These could easily take up half the night. Finishing one of these puzzles was usually a family project, done while listening to *Amos 'n' Andy* on the radio. If the puzzle should be a really big one, the best place for it was on a folding card table, so that it could be pushed aside to be worked on again the next night. This was a relaxing pastime, usually taking place in a warm, old-fashioned parlor with velvet curtains faded to a dull gray-green and ancient floors worn shiny and thin by a generation's footsteps long before.

As Christmas drew closer, many flocked to the local chapel. There was always a group from church caroling around the area.

There were also board games, the great-grandparents of the many games children find today under their Christmas trees. The original board game was probably Parcheesi, a very popular family game for winter evenings.

Evenings preceding Christmas were often spent stringing chains of fluffy white popcorn and bright red cranberries—an economical and homemade decoration for the Christmas tree. The tree itself was found in the spreading, wooded fields near the farmhouse, and was cut with great gusto and joy—a task enjoyed by all.

As the holiday drew closer, many flocked to the local chapel. There was always a group from church caroling around the area. On Christmas Eve the church members would prepare for a visit from Santa, who always arrived by sleigh when everyone was gathered. He always had tall tales to tell about his trip, including incidents that took place getting down some of their chimneys. As a child, I marveled at the way Santa seemed to know everyone in our small community.

After the holidays came the gray skies with white snow falling. This was the time to pull the sleighs from the covered sheds, hitch up the broad-hipped gray mare and take rides on the country roads, now heavy with snow, to visit more friends and relatives. On the way we would marvel at the sparrow tracks, like featherstitching in the snow. The trees glittered like crystal chandeliers, and our words were recorded in breath-script on the icy air.

Other days we spent at the nearby ponds, now heavy with ice. For many months we had been looking forward to skating, and now we glided like feathers blown across the slippery, glassy surface. Later we would cut a hole in the ice to fish, and take our catch home for supper. Even the winter night was a thing of beauty, its heavens scattered with stars.

As cold winter faded and evenings became warmer, the family would again visit neighbors, or get together on Saturday nights to visit the local moving-picture house. We watched comedies with Mary Pickford, Harold Lloyd and Fatty Arbuckle, or dramas with Reginald Denny and Mabel Normand. But best of all were the serials with Ruth Roland, which always left the viewers in suspense. We never failed to return the following Saturday night to see if Pearl White had been rescued from the railroad track where the villain had left her tied for the entire week! Even Jack Dempsey had a serial and boxed every week for our entertainment.

As spring approached, a washed blue sky turned brilliant and the sun grew hotter as it looked down upon those now raking their yards tidy and ripping weeds from their flower beds. We listened to the liquid fluting of the meadowlark and watched hawks circling above. On the ground, we caught a glimpse of a ground squirrel's face and a flash of a chipmunk's stripes. In the woods where we often explored under the dark pines and firs, a fairy slipper bloomed, the most delicate of

wood orchids, and millions and trillions of tiny wildflowers thrust their heads out of the earth as the hard, cold hand of winter lifted.

With the arrival of May we hung up baskets filled with goodies for friends, teachers and neighbors. In June, when the trees wore their summer tresses and the woods in the vale were garbed in dark green gowns, we surprised our friends again with June boxes. And in the muggy heat of July, we would venture out in the cool night to further surprise them with July horns.

Soon summer would be over. The woods now ached and sagged, crying with color, and the bumblebee made haste, since the goldenrod was fast dying. We too made haste to gather the chestnuts falling from their satin burrs, and the red apples lying in piles like jewels shining. We noted the red leaves of woodbine twining on the old stone walls as we breathed in the fragrance of grapes in the lane and the perfume of gentians with fringes rolled tight.

As the wide, gray skies darkened into a late-October night, we would dress up for the long-awaited Halloween night. We would usually spend the late afternoon scooping the pulp and seeds from round, orange pumpkins. These we carried with us at night, a lighted candle inside illuminating the gruesome, grinning faces we had carved. "Tricks and treats" had never been heard of in those days. We celebrated by keeping our jack-o'-lanterns lit, trying to scare our neighbors, and going from door to door, impressing everyone with our homemade costumes.

The tricks we played were quite different than those of today. We didn't consider them too serious. What difference did it make if we tipped over an outhouse, or redesigned clothes left hanging on a line? And I'm sure that tipping the trolleys off their tracks in

nearby towns didn't inconvenience anyone! For many, Halloween was the favorite holiday of the year, celebrated with humorous mischief by young and old alike.

Next came Thanksgiving, a quiet holiday spent eating—not too different from today, except that the food was much less expensive. Most of it had been raised on our own farms, the turkeys, ducks and geese being locally grown. The pumpkin pies were always baked in deep-dish granite pans, and hot, meaty mincemeat pies, which usually sufficed for supper, were nourishing and tasty.

Now we would again face the long winter months, with another Christmas ahead and all that followed.

So if you ever wonder what people did for entertainment in the old days, ask an older person who remembers. You will share their many memories— "when we used crushed Christmas balls for glitter … when the only wish was for a clear night to wish upon a star … when our diaries held our innermost dreams … when we made cookies on rainy days … when all the blues drifted away and smiles invaded our mouths at the corners."

Those of an older generation hold these memories deep in their souls and hearts to cherish. They hold no grief, but gladly share them with anyone who is interested in what happened in yesteryear. ❖

The Party Girl

By Dolores Donegan

Thirty birthday parties in one year—it was the most memorable time of my childhood! In the third grade, one lived for these occasions. If I overheard someone talking about a party, I immediately became a fast friend in order to wangle an invitation. Sometimes strong-arm tactics were necessary—"If you invite me to your party, I'll invite you to mine"—and it generally worked.

Trotting off gaily to each party, I carried a ribbon-tied present, which would be received eagerly by the honoree at her front door.

Excitement mounted as the aroma of hot chocolate drifted through the house. Later it was served with a white, oozing, melting marshmallow in the top of each cup. Ah …

No party was complete without playing Pin the Tail on the Donkey. A picture of a tail-less donkey hung rather limply on the wall and each child, blindfolded, tried to pin a cloth tail on the animal.

The highlight of the year was the party at the home of the only banker in the neighborhood. This was important enough to warrant a new party dress.

Having played the game so often, I found it easy, with a little strategy, to win the prize. When the cloth was tied over my eyes, I would wince and complain that my eyes were sore and the cloth was too tight. It would be loosened just enough to enable me to see the feet of everyone around—and also the spot where the tail belonged. The rest was easy. I pretended to grope my way around the room, but I always managed to win.

The system worked until the day when, at the height of the game, one of my friends said, "No use for us to play. Dolores always wins." Suddenly I realized I had overplayed my hand. Then, with the childish need to be liked by my peers, I changed my tactics; thereafter I managed to get laughs by pinning the tail on the mother's sleeve.

Another game was Hidden Peanuts. Before the guests arrived, a large number of peanuts in the shell were hidden in the living room. As soon as I arrived, I used my experienced eye to seek out places where the nuts might have been hidden. They were concealed everywhere—on windowsill corners, behind drapes and in upholstered chairs. When the mother announced in her sweet party voice, "Now children, we will have a peanut hunt and the one who finds the most will win a prize," I raced around the room like a lighted firecracker, collecting the largest crop. But gathering peanuts eventually became boring, and I learned it was more fun to help the younger children and listen to their squeals of delight.

One freckled-faced girl had a unique party, which led to embarrassment and a bit of sadness for all of us. Jessie's home on the other side of the tracks was sparsely furnished. There were no planned games, but the children had a wonderful run of the house with much shouting and pushing.

The mother, in a grease-stained dress, was evidently exhausted from preparing the menu. She had labored all morning to make a dishpan of warm, salty potato chips. During the afternoon her florid, flushed face indicated some healthy nipping of the sherry bottle and she became nervous and irritable. The climax of the day was a humiliating scene, when the mother, nerves frayed beyond control, started to scream at her daughter and proceeded to give her a spanking. Holding her over a fat knee, with the child's white starched panties exposed to view, she delivered the punishment before a circle of awed little friends.

In contrast to that painful episode, the highlight of the year was the party at the home of the only banker in the neighborhood. This was important enough to warrant a new party dress. So great was my desire to attend this social event that I quickly recovered from an illness, even though I had to disguise a few leftover marks of chicken pox on my chest.

The birthday girl was a beauty, and exceptionally polite. My family would have been surprised at my own angelic behavior and good manners. Instead of the usual party favors of crepe-paper cups filled with hard candy, each child was given a woven straw basket containing real chocolates. The menu consisted of fruit salad in orange shells, hot chocolate with real whipped cream, Nabisco wafers and a serving of decorated cake with two scoops of ice cream. I had second helpings of dessert, and I remember that good, uninhibited feeling of satisfaction I enjoyed as I waddled home.

But I lost my appetite after a rather scary episode at another party. Mollie's folks were good, honest, progressive people, but their beloved child was slow to learn. Having inherited her father's strong features, she was not a raving beauty. From a bulging forehead, her straight black hair was pulled tightly back and braided in a short pigtail. But she was my friend and the best stickball player in the school.

Recently Mollie had been operated on for appendicitis, and during the afternoon she invited a few close friends into her bedroom to see her incision. It was a ghastly sight! With my heart beating like a sledgehammer, I inspected the reddish brown scar, which ran the length of her stark white stomach and was decorated with stitch marks. It resembled a gorgeous tattoo.

After the shock wore off, I began to wonder how I could acquire such a fine decoration. Perhaps it could be copied with red ink, or Crayolas.

It is said one never outgrows his or her childhood pleasures and delights. How wonderful were the years when the words "cholesterol" and "calories" had no meaning!

Today is my birthday. My husband and I will celebrate by dining at a fancy French restaurant. I'll have the clear soup, a skinless piece of unsalted chicken, polyunsaturated vegetables and decaffeinated coffee. Then I'll enjoy a heavenly, delicious, exquisite piece of German chocolate cake. I can hardly wait! I'm still a Party Girl! ❖

Happy Unbirthday!

By Lili Kivisto

I think I'll never forget the year that I had no birthday party. When my sisters and I were growing up, birthdays were normally special occasions. Since my younger sister Trina's birthday and mine were just three weeks apart, we usually had a joint gala celebration. This year, however, the annual event was not to be.

It started with chicken pox in the middle of September. "Oh, it's nothing serious," the doctor told my mother when Betty (my oldest sister), Trina and I all came down with the infectious disease. "Just keep them inside and make sure they don't come in contact with other children."

"What about our party?" Trina and I both wailed. It was just one short week until Trina's birthday and all our party plans had been made.

"Hush," Mom said. "You'll be over chicken pox by then, or if not, we can just hold it later."

Betty recovered first and went back to school. The next day, however, she brought home a case of the mumps. We all caught it, of course, and recovered, only to fall victim to swollen glands, measles and so many colds all winter that Mom was too busy to even think of a party. By spring, Trina and I had resigned ourselves to the idea that "later" would be a whole year away, and that the only party we could look forward to was Betty's birthday bash in the middle of summer.

Now, a year can seem like a very long time to a child. My mother must have realized this, because in April she gathered Trina and me together and asked if we wanted to have a party.

"A birthday party?" Trina asked.

"No, that wouldn't be appropriate," my mother said, "but how would you kids like to have a Hard Times Party? Goodness knows, we've had a hard enough time of it this past winter."

"What's a Hard Times Party?" we wanted to know.

My mother told us that it dated back to the time she was a girl. For a Hard Times Party, guests dressed in their oldest clothes. Refreshments were served off of tin plates and cups, and there was a prize for the person who looked most "down on his luck."

We sent out the invitations, telling everyone to dress down instead of up. What fun my friends had, getting their "costumes" ready for the party! Ragbags were searched for appropriate attire; here was the perfect excuse to wear the sock with a hole for a big toe or a baseball cap three sizes too small. Attics were raided and fathers' uniforms appeared again in all their faded glory. Bandanas, floppy hats, patched blue jeans with rope belts—we were quite a sight the day we assembled for the party.

It started with a parade to show the neighborhood our costumes in all their splendor. People whispered and smiled as they watched from their front porches. Then we moved to the back yard to play "unbirthday" games, the kind that would be forbidden at a more conventional party: Red Rover, Frozen Tag, Red Light, Green Light—action games where we let ourselves be free. No parent minded, since we were wearing our oldest clothes.

Then it was time for refreshments. Hungrily we dug into sloppy joes masquerading as "hobo stew." We drank down our ade from sterilized lemonade cans and ate our "Depression cake" from paper plates on the picnic table in the backyard. Then we threw everything—costumes, plates and all—into the trash, and continued playing shadow tag until the sun went down.

Today I often think back to that party and compare it with the ones children attend today. Every child comes dressed in his best, with mothers, aunts and grandparents carefully in attendance to see that no child gets the slightest bit dirty. All the games are carefully supervised, and at the end, everyone sits down to a piece of store-bought cake.

Did I miss so much not having a birthday party that year? Looking back, that Hard Times Party was the best birthday—or *un*birthday party—a kid ever had! ❖

Fun on a Flying Jenny

By Isole Townsend Baker

In my early childhood, parents had never heard of a weekly allowance for children. Money to rattle in the pocket was unusual. But kids in my family did not need an allowance or a guidebook to find something interesting to do or see. I remember my childhood years in Durant, Okla., as being filled with all the ingredients that make up happiness.

Even without store-bought toys, there was no end to our resources for a good time. In fact, it was often more fun making the toys and making sure they would work than it was playing with them.

One day my father made us a flying jenny. When he had to cut down a large tree in the front yard, he left the stump about 2½ feet tall. Across it he placed a 2 x 12 board with a hole bored through the center. Then, using a sledge-hammer, he drove a heavy iron pin through the hole and down into the stump.

One of us children got on each end of the board, as if on a seesaw, and the third pushed us around until the flying jenny had enough speed to keep going when he jumped out of its path.

My brothers each had sidewalk scooters, which they had made—and I often borrowed. They made their scooters by fastening the wheels from an old roller skate to each end of an 18-inch 2 x 4 board. At the front end they nailed another board upright at a right angle, reaching about waist high. Across the upright board they attached a smaller board for handle-bars. A tin-can headlight was optional deluxe equipment. The rider kept one foot on the scooter while the other foot furnished the locomotion.

The only problem was that since we lived where country and town overlapped, we had no sidewalk in our immediate neighborhood. But what are a couple of blocks to children? We could walk the scooter to the sidewalk. Then we could push off and sail all the way to our dad's grocery store downtown, just seven blocks.

We all had stilts, too. My first ones were empty tin cans with the open end facing the ground. On the closed end, two holes were punched with an ice pick. Then baling wire was measured from the outside hole up to my cupped hand, back down through the other hole, and the ends of the wire were twisted underneath. With a foot on top of each can, I learned to raise one foot at a time, cautiously take a step forward, then carefully move the other foot. What an achievement for a small child!

When I could walk fairly well on my can stilts, I graduated to wooden ones made by my older brother. They had wooden, wedge-shaped footrests securely fastened to two long, sturdy boards. The footrests were raised higher and higher as the stilt-walker became more expert and daring. Mine were usually nearer the ground than my brothers'.

Our neighborhood friends, the three Boner girls, and I were all tomboys, climbing all the trees in the orchard. One afternoon we were playing house, each living in a separate tree. Bill, my older brother, came running to the orchard, yelling, "Quick, run to the cellar! A tornado is coming! Hurry!"

Not looking to see that the sky was clear blue with not a cloud in sight, I jumped for the ground. But my dress-tail and petticoat caught on a stub where a limb had broken off, and I was left dangling in midair, like a spider hanging from a web.

Mother heard me yelling and ran to my rescue. By the time she discovered my plight, Bill had disappeared. She had to get a stepladder to get me down.

Whether we were whirling on the flying jenny, climbing trees, or enjoying any of a dozen other things, none of us children ever complained, "There's nothing to do!" ❖

Dad & the Roller Skate Club

By Loyce E. Billingham

et's go roller-skating!" was the happy cry of so many growing-up years.

And back then, the word was "skating." We'd never heard of "blading"; only ice skates had blades. And only ice skates had shoes. Roller skates had four wheels mounted on a foot-shaped metal platform with a small projecting rod. This platform was clamped onto the skater's shoe, then tightened in place by means of a hollow key slipped over the rod. Using the key, the skates could be adjusted in length and width—and even the most scatter-brained child guarded that key. If that precious key was lost, the skates could only be adjusted with pliers—a tedious process and, in a child's hands, not always effectual.

Their adjustability made roller skates a blessing to parents in the Depression years. A pair of rollers made a gift for two or three children of similar size, and then could be handed down. So during those gray years of 1930–1933, whatever else children might have lacked in toys and play equipment, we all had roller skates.

Using the key, the skates could be adjusted in length and width—and even the most scatter-brained child guarded that key.

Remember the lilting song of the skates—that *zinging* sound that was almost music? Remember the vibration in the soles of your feet while you were skating and long after you had removed the skates? What a wonderful sensation!

My dad was an honorary member of our skaters' club. Dad was a crackerjack salesman—weatherstripping and insulation—but there was a long, dark time when no one was buying anything that wasn't absolutely necessary. Fortunately, Dad had many friends, and one of them owned (and managed to hold on to) a small chain of gas stations.

When the gentleman caught the manager of the station on our corner cheating on the receipts, he fired the offender and offered Dad the job. It was hardly a demanding one, since people who still owned cars could afford gas only for strictly essential driving. This may have been—and no doubt was—a worry to my parents, but it was great for my friends and me.

Our skating route started at the corner station. We'd adjust our skates while sitting on the steps and then take off! Down the wide sidewalk on Hope Street we'd go, around the corner into Rose Street, down the narrower sidewalk there, around another corner into Center Street and, three abreast, down Center Street, where there were no sidewalks, but just about no traffic, either.

Around the sharp corner into Scofield Avenue we skated, single file down the narrow Scofield Avenue sidewalk, back to Hope Street and the gas station. Sometimes we skated across Hope—carefully, as this was the only street with traffic—and then whizzed around the triangle on that side, into Colonial Road, into Puritan Lane, and back to Hope Street.

With business so slow, Dad had time to help new tyros adjust skates and steady them 'round and 'round the station apron while they learned to balance themselves.

He arbitrated the "Whose turn?" squabbles among sharing siblings, gave occasional first aid, and shepherded us across Hope Street. He also let us keep our skate keys, carefully tagged for identification, in his cash drawer.

We had competitions along our route. On Hope Street opposite the gas station we played what we called the "whiz-edge game," where we vied to skate closest to the sidewalk's edge without going off into the vacant lot.

There was no prize for the winner, but there was a penalty for losers, for the lot produced a fine crop of poison ivy, much of it near the sidewalk. Dad—who was often called over to decide the winner—finally put on gauntlets and pulled the stuff out all along the walk. He meant well, but we really didn't appreciate it; skating the edge wasn't the same without that element of danger.

On Rose Street, we had another competition. Halfway down Rose was the home of Mrs. Grump. I don't remember Mrs. Grump's real name, but I remember her thundercloud face glaring from her porch. The game there was called "whiz-hedge," and the object was to see who could skate closest to her hedge without brushing it and thereby getting yelled at.

Inevitably the day came when I not only brushed that hedge but crashed through it. The mishap damaged me more than the hedge, but that didn't pacify Mrs. Grump. First she yelled, then she called the station and complained to Dad, who quoted her what he said was a town ordinance—and maybe it was—requiring property owners to keep shrubbery trimmed back from public walkways.

And, while sticking Band-Aids over my wounds, he also quoted us his opinion of children who tormented elderly neighbors, grumpy or not. Thus we were shamed into abandoning whiz-hedge. It wasn't much of a sacrifice, as it turned out; we soon found that the game was over anyway. On our way home that very day, we found Mr. Grump vigorously, if ineptly, plying the hedge shears.

As the Great Depression ground along its weary way, frustration sometimes turned to desperation. One evening, just as Dad was locking up, a man with his collar pulled up and slouch hat pulled down burst through the door and accosted Dad.

This unknown pointed a gun at poor Dad (who afterward complained to the police that "He wasn't even polite about it!"), threw a canvas bag on the counter and demanded the contents of the cash register. Dad promptly complied.

I wish I could have seen the thief's reaction when he counted his take. Business being what it was, he certainly didn't get much money. What he did get was a great haul of roller skate keys!

From that day on, Dad spent a lot of time for our skate club on his knees, busy with pliers. ❖

© *Skating Party* by John Sloane

Skating

By Sally Cochran

On clear, crackling days
We bundled up in woolens,
Slung skates about our necks
Like garlands,
And set out to celebrate
The cold.

We trudged through snowy fields,
Laughing as you sank hip-deep
In my knee-high steps.
We clambered over fences,
Bold as Viking invaders
Swooping down on innocent towns,
Ducked low-slung branches
And crossed the dirt road
To the hidden pond
Protected by guardian pines.

We hurried on our skates,
Swearing at knotty laces,
And blew on frozen fingertips
As if we were about to roll a winner.

Then we raced about the ice,
Avoiding snowy places near shore,
Swirled in and out
Among sticks and trunks
Poking like broken bones
Through taut, shiny skin—
Mad dervishes
Spurred on by arctic air.

The wind-swept center
Was as clean as a blackboard
On the first day of school
Until we sullied it
With careless scrawls
That would soon be erased.

Once warmed,
We slowed our pace,
And there in that lonely place,
We skated out our dreams
To the leisurely rhythm
Of the wind harp's tune.

© John Sloane

Our Playground: The Wide Outdoors

By Anne Lucas

On sunny Saturday mornings, all is quiet in our neighborhood. The children are indoors, some watching television, others matching wits with the family computer. Teenagers withdraw to their bedrooms to play music on the stereo.

There was no such expensive hardware around when I was growing up back in the Good Old Days. In fact, few of our toys were store-bought. Further, we were up and outdoors as much as possible, especially on sunny Saturday mornings. What fun we had!

I remember our old backyard, and how proud we were to entertain our playmates there. The swing, made from a rubber tire and a length of chain rescued from the town dump, hung from a bough of the big apple tree and was considered marvelous, because it could also spin in circles as well as go back and forth like ordinary swings.

Our seesaw was a plank balanced over a low stump, and was usually ridden by the older children standing up. Wooden rain barrels lent themselves to many games and pranks. Tall haystacks in an adjoining field made precipitous slides or sites for king-of-the-hill. Near the fence, the crotch of a massive maple supported our ramshackle tree house, made of odds and ends of gray weathered boards. Its walls were only waist-high and it had no roof, so we crouched down when holding secret club meetings, but stood and pranced when it was serving

1932 Procter & Gamble Soap ad, House of White Birches nostalgia archives

as the deck of a pirate ship, or a wooden fort besieged by the enemy.

Farther afield there were challenging trees to climb, birds' nests to peer into (but not touch), wild berries and nuts to gather, a creek to wade in search of crayfish, tadpoles and Indian arrowheads—or for gold nuggets, when we played at Wild West.

Perhaps the favorite game of skill among boys was marbles. How long has it been—30 years?—since I have seen that familiar circle scratched in the earth with a stick, the ground smoothed and cleared of pebbles, the eager boys ringing the arena, waiting their turn to knuckle down with a steelie or an agate?

No boy of our acquaintance ever *bought* marbles. You borrowed a handful off a friend, or inherited the collection of an older brother who had graduated to hanging around the pool hall or tinkering with old cars. Once you were in the game of marbles, since you got to keep your winnings, you might become the town champion, like my brother Bob, who amassed a quart-jar full of rainbow-hued beauties.

The equivalent game of skill for girls was jacks, which I was not very good at. My preference was the jump rope. Here again, you didn't need cash; a fine jump rope could be made from old clothesline. In fact, this was an advantage because the rope could be made longer so that two or three girls could jump at once while two others swung the rope. The rhythmic thud of the rope followed by feet hitting the ground lent itself to gleeful chanting. Most of our chants ended with:

Akka bakka soda cracker,
Akka bakka boo,
Out goes us
And in goes you!

At this point the inside girls jumped out and, without missing a beat, the newcomers jumped in. If some unfortunate did trip, we only laughed and started counting again. (Recently I acquired a jump rope to get myself in shape; frankly, I don't know how we girls ever had the breath to jump and chant too!)

Larger mixed groups played plenty of games that needed no equipment. Hide-and seek was fun when cousins came to visit our farm. Hay-mows, corn shocks, root cellars and the old hollow tree were all good hiding places, as was the gully behind the chicken coop. Mother often told us girls not to hide with a boy cousin because he might pinch, which was a habit some boys had.

I never did hide with a boy on purpose, but once my cousin Gordon dove into my hidey-hole in the lilac thicket. He didn't pinch me, but he did slice off a curl from over my forehead with his penknife. (Most boys carried penknives in those days; they came in handy for leaving initials on trees, cutting a fishing pole, carving a basswood whistle or just plain whittling—and they might even save your life sometime!) Anyway, he nipped off the lock—not for a lover's keepsake, but just to show me how sharp the blade was.

That was one game I didn't finish. I bolted to my room to survey the damage, and cried. The only way to conceal the missing curl seemed to be by cutting bangs. They wouldn't hang straight, so I snipped first on one side, then on the other. I ended up with bangs that were only an inch long and stood out like a ski slide.

Another game, Foxie, was for some reason played only during school recess. In the school-yard, "safe" places were under the shade of an oak tree at one side and the area beyond the edge of the schoolhouse at the other. The child elected as Fox stood in the center and challenged:

"Fox in the morning."

"Geese and the gander!" came the volleying response.

"How many's coming?"

"More than you can handle!"

At that, we Geese ran frantically across the Fox's perilous domain, touched the oak, and then headed back. If you were tagged, you, too, became a Fox, and chased the Geese from then on. The last child to be tagged, hailed as the Gander, often became the Fox for the next day's game.

Even coming home from school provided adventure for us. Chores were waiting and we could not dally, but it was exciting to "follow the leader," usually my oldest brother, Bob. His way led across vacant lots choked with weeds and tall hollyhocks, past a "haunted" house where we peered in timidly through the cracks of boarded-up windows, into the old walled graveyard where lichen-stained tombstones leaned, and across open fields.

Avoiding adult conveniences like roads and bridges, we crossed Chest Creek on stepping-stones, cut through tangled woods, jumped ditches and slid under barbed-wire fences. A detour carried us to the railroad tracks, where we progressed by stepping on every other wooden tie, or by walking a metal rail. As we neared home, the way led up one side of a giant, low-limbed beech tree and down the other side (after each of us had thrust a hand into the dark old squirrel's hole to see if any mysterious messages had been left for us by the James brothers or Billy the Kid).

Yes, we sometimes arrived home tired, with wet feet or scratches and bruises, but we were proud of our exploits and hardiness, too. Colorful imagination—stultified in the modern generation by the dreadful literalness of television—played an important role in our childhood games. The companionship of my sisters, brothers, cousins and playmates from families who were usually just as poor as we were increased our enjoyment of a world that combined make-believe, a love of nature, and the practical ability to devise toys from any discarded household item.

When I think of today's youth huddling indoors in their leisure time, each alone with a machine, I wonder if they realize what they are missing. ❖

Our Favorite Things

Chapter Four

*Raindrops on roses and whiskers
on kittens;
Bright copper kettles and
warm woolen mittens;
Brown paper packages tied up
with strings;
These are a few of my favorite things.*

The words by Oscar Hammerstein and Richard Rodgers from *The Sound of Music* always make me smile and make me think back to the Good Old Days and some of my favorite things.

Probably my "favoritest" thing—as I would say to Mama and Daddy—was my little red wagon. I wish I could remember if mine was a Radio Flyer, but I can't. It's been too long gone now. But if it wasn't, that didn't really matter to me. It was one of the first store-bought, new toys I can ever remember receiving.

My wagon went with me on all the adventurous excursions of youth. It carried all the paraphernalia of boyhood as we moved from one fantasy to another.

I fashioned ribs from short, limber tree branches and begged a piece of material from Mama's sewing. My wagon became a covered wagon and we were traveling west in frontier days. I had my six-shooter at my side and my trusty steed led the imaginary team pulling the prairie schooner. There were, of course, many obstacles along the way. We had to cross rivers (mud holes) and mountains (the hill behind our house) along the way. Once in a while a kind stranger (Grandma, who lived a few hundred yards down the road) would offer a weary traveler a resting place, water and maybe even a cookie, if I was lucky.

Then the scene changed. Now my wagon was a tank and we were busting through enemy lines fighting to free France from the enemy. The few lead soldiers I had lay protected inside my tank until it was time to stop and form battle lines. In the ensuing firefight, I was usually mortally wounded, but somehow found the strength to stumble home where Mama nursed me back to health over dinner.

As I got a bit older, I sought more thrills from my little red wagon. I climbed in the wagon bed and my brother or sister pushed me to dizzying speeds down the hill. With the wagon tongue now hinged into my lap as a steering device, I became a race car driver in the Indianapolis 500, zooming down the final straightaway to take the checkered flag.

Then I discovered on these daring races that a quick push of the tongue to the right or left would send me tumbling in a terrifyingly exciting crash. That spelled doom for my little red wagon, which soon was damaged beyond repair.

Whatever your "favoritest" thing was—whether wagon or doll, cap gun or carriage—I'm sure it carried you to the same world of fantasy mine did. How could we ever have made our own fun without a few of our favorite things?

—*Ken Tate*

House Call by Charles Freitag, courtesy of Apple Creek Publishing

Our Little Dolls

By Doris C. Crandall

*I*t's amazing what old-timers pine for when sighing fondly over the Good Old Days. Daddy yearned for his Model-A for many years after he'd traded up to newer cars. And Mother, with a faraway look in her hazel eyes, often mentioned that she had enjoyed watching the sun rise over the cotton patch when she was a child. I cherish the memory of playing "little dolls" with my younger sister.

Dolly and I started our little doll families when Grandma Bradstreet gave us a set of three dolls: a bride, a groom and a preacher. Since Mother always made us share, I got the groom, Dolly got the preacher and our older sister, Estelle, got the bride.

The dolls were about five inches tall, made of china, and had painted-on hair, facial features and clothes. We named them George, Martha and Preacher. George wore a bridegroom's tails and high hat. Preacher wore a robe and held an open Bible. Martha was dressed in a long white frock with a veil and carried a bridal bouquet.

But Estelle was too old to play with dolls, so she put Martha away in her dresser drawer. Dolly and I determined to buy wives for George and Preacher. The problem was where to get a nickel.

Our dolls with their furniture: two chairs with matching table, candelabrum and chamber pot.

In those days, on our farm, we had plenty of work to do, and we each had assigned chores for which we neither expected nor received pay. But on Saturdays, if we had worked especially hard, Mother would give us each a dime from her cream and egg money. We usually spent it on a matinee to see Roy Rogers or Gene Autry.

One Saturday Dolly said, "Let's not go to the show. Let's buy little dolls." So we went to the variety store, purchased two lady dolls and pretended they married George and Preacher.

Later Aunt Ella gave us a Mother Goose doll (we often received one gift among us), which we dubbed grandma to both families. The fact that "Grandma" permanently carried a goose under one arm didn't bother us at all.

Because we now had Grandma, George and Preacher and their wives, they simply must have children. Then someone gave us a complete set of 10 tiny dolls called "Children of Other Lands." They were just the right size to be the two couples' offspring.

Dolly and I named them (appropriately but not imaginatively) "Chinese Girl," "Indian Boy," "Dutch Boy," etc., according to their nationality. We loved them all equally and, in our thoughts, they lived together in peace as we knew families should.

Wherever we played, we set up housekeeping

Here is the truck our little dolls drove to the baptizing at the water tank.

for our little doll families. Most of the time it was under the lilac bush in the yard. There, we pretended to build their houses by drawing lines on the ground. Later we acquired a doll-size bed, two small chairs and a table to match, a candelabrum, a lamp and a tiny chamber pot.

By the same method we "built" a church, a general store and a school so we could pretend the children went to school, the parents got the mail at the general store as Mother and Daddy did, and they all attended church.

Through Dolly's voice, Preacher preached and George—through me—led the song service. While pretending George was singing, I waved one hand and flattened my nose with a finger of the other so I'd resemble the flat-nosed song leader in the real country church we attended.

Our favorite songs were *When the Roses Call Up Yonder* (our mistake) and *Amazing Grace*, though we sometimes tossed in a few choruses of *Yo, Ho, We'll*

Since the dolls couldn't bend, they had to sit like this.

Blow the Man Down, which we had learned in school. And we weren't above belting out a song our parents never allowed us to sing in their presence called *I'll Be Glad When You're Dead, You Rascal, You.*

I had a red metal toy truck with yellow wooden wheels that we made believe belonged to our little dolls. After a simulated revival meeting, the dolls jumped into the truck and drove the long distance to the horse tank at the windmill where Preacher baptized them. We did that so often that their painted faces and clothes faded. Finally, we could barely make out the color of their eyes, but we didn't mind.

Our doll families didn't cuss, drink alcoholic beverages or smoke cigarettes. They didn't use drugs and they never committed a crime. The grown-ups voted in every election. On Wednesday nights they attended prayer meeting, and they went to church twice on Sunday.

They worked hard from Monday through Saturday noon, and then got to town before the bank closed at 2 p.m. The men, like our father, had to borrow money to buy food and medicine for another month. Bankers loaned the money with future crops as collateral.

Dolly and I sometimes disagreed over what the doll families would do on a particular day. But we both knew sisters were harder to replace than dolls, so we usually resolved our differences without resorting to having to call Mother and say, "Mother, make her …"

Not long ago I found a shoebox tucked away way back in the closet. It contained most of the little dolls, though George and Preacher were missing. I still have the truck, the furniture and some of the "Children of Other Lands."

When I think about the world as it is today, with neighbor fighting neighbor, memories of that little doll world Dolly and I dreamed up, where people of all races lived and worshiped together peacefully, flood my mind and delight my heart.

Yes, older people yearn for some amazing things they recall from the Good Old Days. I say, "To each his own." Memories are precious. They live in our hearts and minds, waiting to whisper back to us to give us strength and hope, or simply touch us with affection. ❖

Peggy the Clothes-Peg Doll

Editor's Note: *Often we see clothes-peg dolls living in dollhouses. By adding trims, aprons and lace, each doll can be different. The hair is painted on or glued-on yarn or mohair. The face is painted and pipe cleaner arms are glued on.*

To make the skirt, cut a piece of fabric 3 x 5 inches. Fold over the top and run a row of gathering stitches across it. When the bodice is on the doll, slip the skirt over the bodice, tighten the gathering stitches and stitch the back opening closed. Blindstitch the skirt to the bodice. ❖

Old Crackle Face

By Ruby Ida Denton

I don't remember when I got her. She was just an ordinary doll. She was nothing like the beautiful porcelain dolls of today.

Her body was cloth, stuffed with sawdust. Her head, arms, hands, feet and lower legs were made from composition, the material from which dolls of the 1930s and '40s were most commonly made. Her little round face was brightened by her permanent painted smile and her rosy cheeks.

I don't remember what I named her when Santa Claus first left her for me. I only remember what I called her after her accident.

Work was the core of life on our northeast Texas farm and left little time for play. Farm payments and expenses left little money for nonessentials. But Santa Claus somehow found a way to put a new member of my doll family under the tree each Christmas.

My family of dolls began before I can remember and grew each year. By the time I was 12, I had 13 dolls. With each new addition, I cherished them more. Playtime usually found us outdoors in the shade of a chinaberry tree in the backyard. There I'd "build" a playhouse, drawing walls in the sand with a stick, collecting pieces of wood for furniture, and playing with whatever odds and ends of empty bottles, cans or other items I could salvage from the kitchen.

Our East Texas weather was as changeable as a chameleon. Winter days could quickly change from balmy conditions to near freezing if a norther blew in. Summer days could change from bright and sunny to a heavy rainstorm with little warning. It was on such a day that my doll met her accident.

Mother had warned me repeatedly about leaving my dolls outside, lest the elements ruin them. On this particular day, for some reason I had only the one doll outside in the playhouse with me.

I had just put her to bed on her plank bed when Mother called me to come in for supper. As I rushed in the door, Mother reminded me, "You need to bring in your doll. It may rain tonight." But to my six-year-old mind, this was unnecessary worrying. I saw no sign of rain.

"I will after I eat," I said. "She's sleeping." Then I promptly forgot about her.

When I awoke the next morning, rain was dripping from the eaves of the old house and puddles stood all over the yard. Then I remembered. Quickly I put on my clothes and ran to the back yard, fearful of what I would find.

True to my fears, there was my pretty little doll, still lying on her plank bed. But her rose face was all cracked and peeling! Big tears rolled down my face and dripped onto her wet, ruined face. "Oh!" I cried as I hugged her close. "My poor old Crackle Face!"

The sun came out and I laid her out to dry, but the results were worse. As the cracked composition dried, the painted pieces fell off, leaving only the hard, black material onto which the composition had been bonded. Crackle Face looked awful and I felt awful.

Ever after, she was "Old Crackle Face." She stayed around for many years, a silent reminder of my thoughtlessness. But I loved her, perhaps even more than the others who kept their pretty faces, because she had been part of a painful lesson. We had been happy together, and we had suffered together, she and I. Is that not, after all, what love is all about? ❖

The Ups & Downs Of Yo-Yos

By Deborah J. Beyer

Skimming through the pages of the weighty holiday toy catalog, I stopped. There, amidst the solar-powered helicopters and transformable moving robots (batteries not included), was an old friend. Although I hadn't seen one in years, it hadn't changed a bit. It was a chunky wooden yo-yo like one I'd used in the early 1950s.

This yo-yo boasted no ball bearings, lights or tinsel spinners, like so many of its modern relatives. It didn't hum, whistle or otherwise make a sound. It wasn't spring-loaded to guarantee return. It wasn't fashioned of glistening metal or neon plastic. It was just a wooden yo-yo, homely and plain. But for me it was loaded with something more important than ball bearings and flickering lights. It was loaded with memories.

As a child, I lived near a municipal playground with a supervised summer program. A highlight of each summer was a visit from the yo-yo man. He was often a college student who traveled from playground to playground and mesmerized us with his skill.

I've since learned that these traveling spellbinders were part of the Duncan Yo-Yo Company's postwar promotion campaign for its product. Requirements to be a yo-yo man were few but important: adeptness with the toy, a touch of showmanship and mountains of patience for little ones.

We watched the annual performance, fascinated by the skill of the yo-yo man—or perhaps bewitched by the fantasy that we, too, could become yo-yo stars. We dreamed of making the device dance across the floor, "sleep" and perform the acrobatic tricks of an Olympic gymnast.

After the show, the yo-yo man peddled his toys for $1 each. Each summer we eagerly anted up our dollar bills (or six dimes, two nickels, a handful of pennies and a button), then waited patiently as the salesman carved the name of the purchaser through the bright red, green or blue paint of each toy.

For days, sometimes weeks, we practiced. Then the yo-yo was relegated to a drawer where its string became hopelessly entangled in the miscellany there. But for a brief time, the fantasy was vivid that we, too, could achieve the stunning skill of the playground yo-yo man.

After ordering a yo-yo from the catalog for my youngest son, I read that yo-yos are making a comeback. Duncan Toys, Inc., the largest maker of the toy, had launched a renewed marketing campaign, complete with school science programs using yo-yos to help students explore the principles of potential and kinetic energy. The yo-yo man was back, but with a whole new shtick.

Duncan began manufacturing yo-yos in the 1920s, but the toy has a much longer history. Toys similar to yo-yos originated in China around 1000 B.C.; they consisted of two ivory disks joined by a center peg and spun on a silk cord. Greek artifacts dating to 450 B.C. show a version of the yo-yo as well. A form of the yo-yo was a traditional weapon in the Philippines as early as the 1500s. There, large wooden disks on a heavy cord were thrown at prey, somewhat like the South America bola.

The yo-yo's small size and portability have made it popular for centuries—although in 1993, engineering students at Stockport College in England built the largest recorded version, a whopping 10 feet, 4 inches in diameter, and weighing in at 897 pounds. It was suspended from a 187-foot crane and "yo-yoed" four times.

But there were no giant yo-yos for my son or me. His first was the simple, familiar device of my youth. I've been secretly practicing. I'll never be as good as the yo-yo man, but I might capture my son's attention and admiration for a few minutes. Then I'll step aside while he builds his own brief fantasy life as a professional yo-yo star. ❖

The Pea Shooter

By Francis Xavier Sculley

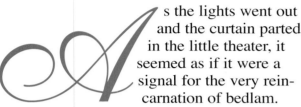

As the lights went out and the curtain parted in the little theater, it seemed as if it were a signal for the very reincarnation of bedlam. Shrieking, stamping, whistling kids drowned out the sound of the opening scenes of the movie.

Suddenly, from out of his sleeve, my companion sneaked out a long tube, one end of which he stuck in his mouth. There was a *splat!* and a bean caromed off the bull's eye 10 rows ahead. The target happened to be a senior citizen, who turned around in righteous wrath.

"Put that away!" I implored him. "Do you want us to get thrown out?" But one taste of success had gone to Richie's head. He was always a leader in any mischief making. Reaching into his pocket, he came out with a fistful of beans. As the suspicious usher stopped by his aisle, the towhead made like he was eating peanuts, and soon had all of the ammunition securely locked in the magazine—his mouth. As the usher moved away, the screen was mysteriously hit with a hail of beans. Instantly the weapon disappeared into Richie's shirt, and he put on an inscrutable mask as the usher stopped by his seat and shined his flashlight into the face of the suspect.

A little later, Richie said, "Here—hold my bean blower. I've got to go to the bathroom." With that, Rich took off for the basement of the tiny theater, leaving me holding the bag.

While the villain of the story was away, I shifted the bean blower from my rear pocket to my shirt, and with that movement, the flashlight flicked on, plainly exposing the weapon. In a moment I was outside the theater, despite all of my pleas of innocence. To make it worse, Rich asked for the return of his blower as the usher led me to the door by the scruff of the neck.

The most famous bean blower or pea shooter of all was the homemade job, which consisted merely of a six-inch section of elder bush with the soft pith pushed from the center with a piece of wire or one of Mom's hatpins. With this simple contrivance, kids of the day could knock a gnat off a poppyseed roll at 50 feet. And green elderberries made the finest ammunition. Some of the kids were so accurate with their shooters that they could make a shambles of an orchestra pit from the back row in the balcony.

Kids even engaged in bean-blowing duels across a classroom while the teacher had her back to the class. The amazing thing was not the accuracy, but rather the speed with which the weapons and ammunition could disappear. Within a second, a halo would appear over the suspect as absolute silence reigned.

Then some astute toymaker came out with a peashooter to end all pea shooters. It was a hollow metal tube about a foot long, with a wooden mouthpiece. It would propel a bean, pea or tiny pebble with the speed of shrapnel, thus making the beloved homemade elderberry shooter obsolete. Kids from far and near plunked down their nickels to buy one of these new weapons, which could torment a saint to mayhem.

So Richie acquired a new metal shooter. It certainly was a beauty, and with his accuracy and guile, the junior high school orchestra led a dog's life for an entire term. One day, however, with his mouth full of birdshot, Richie had to answer to our principal, who had sneaked up behind him. Long suspicious, he finally made his move. When he tapped our hero on the shoulder, Richie couldn't speak with the birdshot in his mouth, so he swallowed it.

Grim retribution. ❖

Double-Ripper Days

By Alfred E. Ross

I don't suppose you have ever heard of a "double-ripper," as it was generally known in the area of New England where I spent my boyhood. At that time long ago, when there were fewer automobiles on the roadways and fewer sophisticated devices available for the amusement of children and young adults, the double-ripper was perhaps the hottest and most popular contrivance ever invented.

As I watched a group of youngsters racing around an open field on their droning snowmobiles, I couldn't help but think how different this winter scene was from that of long ago.

The heavy snowfall of a few days earlier was packed down on the road into a slippery, shimmering surface, and practically all the children in the community were gathered on the hilltop for an after-school frolic. A number of animated boys and girls were sliding down the hill on their little sleds. At the same time, a dozen older children on a big double-ripper went streaking down the long incline, around a curve and onto the village green more than a mile away.

Every conceivable sort of sled was in use. Some were homemade. Others were factory-designed and manufactured. These were of varying sizes and construction, and some—like the Flexible Flyer—were much desired.

But of all the sleds in use, without doubt the double-ripper was the most popular, for it gave its riders many breathtaking moments of excitement and pleasure. Indeed, for a thrilling, hair-raising experience, there was nothing in those days to equal a ride on a double-ripper in the company of some 12 or 13 friends, all hanging on to each other for dear life from their seats behind the husky fellow who was in control. It was an unforgettable sensation accentuated by the tingling bite of the wind and the rhythmic movement of bodies leaning to the right or left with the motion of the steersman as he veered away from an obstacle or negotiated a curve.

It was an unforgettable sensation accentuated by the tingling bite of the wind and the rhythmic movement of bodies leaning to the right or left with the motion of the steersman as he veered away from an obstacle or negotiated a curve.

It was great fun. None of the boys gave heed to the long, hard pull up the hill for another ride down. It was worth the effort and fatigue just to have the thrill and joy of it all once more.

Usually the double-ripper of those days was handcrafted by some enterprising youth. Although it was crude by modern standards of workmanship, it was carefully constructed and skillfully put together with materials strong enough to withstand the most severe strain.

It was guided and held on its course by means of hemp rope securely fastened on either side of the front bobsled. The steersman grasped the rope firmly in each hand, like reins, and by pulling one side or another, it was comparatively easy to maintain stability and control—providing, of course, that all the riders behind him moved in concert when it was necessary to lean.

The earliest double-rippers were nothing much to look at. They were constructed using materials at hand: a pair of homemade bobsleds

Tobagganing by George Brehm © 1926 SEPS: Licensed by Curtis Publishing

identical in size and weight; a 14- or 15-foot, 1-inch hardwood plank; a set of mounting blocks or risers; a set of heavy-duty steel pins; a pair of steel runners (usually forged by the village blacksmith); and a length of stout hemp rope.

The steel pins, which functioned as swivels, passed through the center of the blocks, which were securely fastened to the bobsleds and plank. One of the bobsleds was centered at the rear of the plank, flush with the end. However, in order to provide leverage and control, the front bobsled was set so that the runners extended a couple of feet beyond the front edge of the plank. This arrangement enabled a steersman to control his ripper with little effort.

Generally, double-rippers were never painted or varnished or given a protective covering, such as linseed oil. These details seemed unimportant to those who built them and, of course, they had little meaning for those who indulged in the sport. It did not matter if the plank was hard and cold; one did not feel any discomfort while seated on a fast-moving ripper hurtling down a steep incline. One felt only the firm clasp of the arms of the rider behind him around the waist, and the pleasant sensation of synchronized physical motion when everybody responded to the steersman as he leaned left or right to round a curve or avoid an obstacle in the path.

Of course, there was a thrilling touch of fear mingled with the excitement of riding a double-ripper. No one was ever quite sure that all would go well, and sometimes—though not often—a mishap did occur. At such times, an upset usually sent everyone sprawling, but even so, hardly anyone was ever hurt. In fact, I can recall only one ride when

there was a serious misfortune. That was when a young fellow who had just built and tried out his double-ripper for the first time on an unfamiliar course failed to make a sharp turn and smashed into a tree, breaking his leg. He was the only one of the riders who was hurt. None of the others was even bruised, and as I recall, none lost his enthusiasm for the sport because of that misadventure.

Presumably there would be little to lure boys and girls of school age to a sledding party on a snappy winter afternoon in this day and time. Perhaps the exposure would be too much for them by modern standards of comfort. Perhaps the exertion required to haul a sled from the base of a hill to its starting point would soon tire and disenchant them. Such are the changes that have been wrought in our attitudes over the years since those delightful double-ripper days. ❖

Sturdy, Streamlined
SLED
given to every
Girl and Boy!
It's easy—get yours quick.

Concave Runners
Extra Heavy Knees

Form Fitting Top
Easy Steering

2800 POUNDS

Speed Boat Front
Greater Tested Strength

This fine big sled, Prize No. 345F, will be sent postpaid to every girl and boy for two or more subscription orders for The Farmer's WIFE Magazine amounting to only $2 and you can give 40 months for only $1 or one year for 50 cents.

New and renewal orders may be combined, but you are not allowed to pay for any subscription order yourself.

Streamlined like a speed boat, form fitting top that hugs you on as you whiz around a corner, strong and sturdy as only selected white ash and steel can make it—this sled will tickle every youngster. Attractively decorated and finished with marine spar varnish to withstand the weather. Set-back steering bar that is easy to control with your hands or feet. Concave runners, extra heavy knees, three feet long, tested up to 2,800 pounds. If you want a fine sled, here is your chance to get it quick.

Send to
The Farmer's WIFE Magazine,
St. Paul, Minn.

1939 Pioneer Racer ad, House of White Birches nostalgia archives

Admiral of the Putt-Putts

By Lewis S. English

My children and grandchildren are all adults now, so I seldom stop at toy counters. But when I happened to pass one recently, I paused to take a look. I was amazed at the variety—not to mention the cost—of the toys on display.

As I gazed at those brightly painted, battery-operated, modern toys, I remembered our primitive toys of the 1930s. None of them was costly to operate.

Besides my baseball bat and marbles, I had two favorite toys. One was a wire-framed airplane covered with bright silk gauze and powered by rubber bands. After winding them tightly by turning the propeller with my finger, I tossed the plane into the air. Its flights were short, but it did fly—and that was a big enough thrill enough for me!

But, my *really* favorite toys—and I owned several—were my "Putt-Putt" boats. They first appeared in 1934, at our local five-and-dime store. I got my first one in the spring of that year. It cost 25 cents—big money for a toy in the Depression! And shortly afterward, an uncle and aunt gave me a boxed set of three for my 10th birthday! They ranged in size from about 5 inches in length to perhaps 8 or 10 inches.

I remember opening the package and rushing to fill our bathtub so they could be launched. I liked to get all three running at once, which was hard to do since their "steaming times" were short. But I spent many happy hours with them, playing my role of "bathtub admiral."

Putt-Putts really ran on steam, though they had no "engines" as such. Each boat had a small tin boiler, slightly larger than a postage stamp.

It sat in the bow (forward end) of the boat. From beneath it, two small tubes about 1/8 inch in diameter curved down and back, to stick out through the stern.

To prepare for steaming, I held the boat with bow straight down, and with a small rubber syringe, squirted water into the ends of each pipe until they overflowed. That indicated the boiler was filled. Once the boat was in a tub or pond, the pressure of the outer water kept the boiler from draining. The boiler itself was bent down a bit too, which helped hold the water inside.

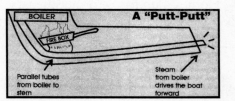

Then I put a dab of Sterno in the boat's firebox, which was a small tin tray with a short handle sticking out behind. This fuel was cheap; Sterno was a form of solidified alcohol, and a large can cost only 10 or 15 cents. Flanges on its bottom (like an inverted letter U) fit over the tubes and kept it in place.

Then I lit the Sterno and shoved the firebox beneath the boiler. After a few seconds, my boat began *putt-putting* along, giving them their name. Unfortunately, their boilers had short lives, so I doubt that many Putt-Putts still exist. But I had many hours of fun with mine!

I suppose few children would be allowed to play with Putt-Putts today, even if they were available. Blistered fingers were an occupational hazard; under today's laws, each boat would have to be sold with a 10-inch-thick operator's manual! And the boat would probably sink anyway, once all the mandatory warning labels had been pasted on it!

Still, I enjoyed playing with my Putt-Putts. And I learned to handle matches very carefully, too! If we had fun with our toys and learned something while we played with them, I'd say we didn't do too badly! Don't you agree? ❖

Toy Soldiers

By Fred W. Kelly Jr.

As a boy in St. Louis during World War II, I was always thrilled to see shiny, new, lead soldiers emerge from the sooty black molds of my home casting set.

On a rainy day, my younger brother, Jack, and I would go down the spiral stairs into our dark basement to a storage locker near our hand-fed coal furnace. After a brief search, we found the box labeled "Lead Casting Set by Home Foundry Mfg., Chicago, Illinois," and took it upstairs to our apartment.

The first thing I did was plug in the small electric ladle, because it took a long time to get hot enough to melt the lead. Jack gathered up our broken and bent lead soldiers, casualties of previous war games. We looked over our selection of molds and chose "The Marines Have Landed."

The electric ladle was now smoking, so we dropped in broken soldiers and watched the arms, legs, and torsos slowly dissolve into liquid gray lead. We added some lead pipes, begged from a local plumbing shop, to fill the pot. As everything melted, I skimmed off the smoking scum of dirt and paint.

Jack screwed wooden handles onto the halves of the aluminum mold, and then we held them low in the flame of the little alcohol lamp from our Gilbert chemistry set to coat them with black soot.

The blackened molds were clamped together, and we waited impatiently for a bluish scum to

Fred's old casting set and some of the lead soldiers he made.

form on the molten lead, which meant it was hot enough to pour. Then I carefully poured the lead into the mold in a steady stream. After a brief wait, Jack pulled the mold out of the clamp and separated the halves.

Opening the mold was the moment of truth. We were usually thrilled to find three complete, shiny lead soldiers lying in the smoky black mold. Sometimes, however, an arm or leg was missing; then the pieces went back into the pot for another try.

We arranged our new soldiers in a battle scene with toy tanks and planes and then got out our ElecToy electric cannon. Jack dropped a wooden bullet down the cannon's black Bakelite barrel. I aimed and set the angle of the barrel, and then pressed the electric button to fire the gun. The electromagnet in the black box at the base of the barrel made a loud bang and shot the wooden projectile across the room into the ranks of shiny lead soldiers.

After a long bombardment, often finished off with a BB-gun barrage, we again had a pile of broken lead soldiers ready to go into the melting pot on another rainy day.

Fifty years later, I still get out my home casting set occasionally just to show the neighborhood kids how we had fun in the Good Old Days. Can anyone imagine a manufacturer selling a toy to kids these days that involves pouring molten lead into aluminum molds that have been smoked over an open flame? ❖

Sling Shots & Ticktacks

By Ken Wise

Remember the toys we played with when we were kids? They sure weren't electronic, push-button, computer-type toys like our grandchildren have today. We were more likely to have homemade Raggedy Ann dolls for girls, and tops and marbles for boys.

My dad made me some American folk toys and I made some for myself. A couple of barrel staves worked well for the rockers to make a rocking horse. Scrap lumber and tree limbs were used for the legs, seat and head with a handle on each side. Once it was finished, away we would rock—"Hi-yo, Silver! Away!"

Almost every country boy had a slingshot. They were easy to make and cost nothing. We would cut a forked branch from a tree and shape it to size with a pocketknife. Then we could find a discarded inner tube and cut a couple of rubber strips about a foot long from it. We tied one end of each strip to one of the forks, and attached the other ends to a leather pocket, perhaps cut from an old boot. Then, with some rocks for "bullets," we were ready to go hunting. I never became a good shot, but some boys could kill a rabbit or gopher with their slingshots.

Believe it or not, my sister (yes, she had a slingshot, too) and I used our slingshots to shoot at telephone poles on our way from Canada to Idaho as we rode in Dad's 1911 Ford, an open-air touring car. At every stop Sis and I scurried to refill our coffee cans with ammunition. Man! There were a lot of telephone poles between Canada and Idaho. And once we passed, a few of those poles bore dents from a well-fired shot from our slingshots.

You probably treasured some special toys of your own. Remember the whirligig, the moon winder or buzz saw, the floating ball or flipperdinger, the Jacob's ladder, the hooey stick or whimmydiddle or gee haw, the rope climber, the limber-jack or dancing man or stomp-er, the flapjack or acrobat, and the ticktack? The toys' names varied from region to region around the country.

Up to a Little Mischief by Jay Killian, House of White Birches nostalgia archives

At Halloween we used the ticktack to startle our neighbors. We held it against the window, then pulled a string wrapped around a notched wooden spool. When the string was released, the ticktack created a heck of a racket, scaring anyone inside. Then we took off; it wasn't "trick or treat" in those days—just "trick and run."

Say! If the kids of today read this, I may be in big trouble for telling about sling-shots and Halloween ticktack tricks. But would kids today leave their computers long enough to make toys? I don't think so.

Change is inevitable, of course, but I am not all that sure that it is always for the best. We oldsters still dream of the Good Old Days when toys weren't the push-button type. I still make all the toys I've mentioned here. At 88 years old, I am still living in the Good Old Days. How lucky can you get? ❖

Wooden Scooters

By William James Ezzo Sr.

A Spiderman motorcycle went by, followed closely by a Batmobile, which in turn was hotly pursued by a CHiPs Cycle, complete with windshield. They rounded the corner out of sight, but the sounds of their make-believe engines came back at me. When they were in full view again, the Batmobile had taken the lead and the child on the Spiderman motorcycle pedaled frantically to retake the position he had previously held, his rainbow-colored streamers flapping in the wind.

As I watched these youngsters at play with their super-hero vehicles, my mind's eye brought forth images of myself playing in much the same manner as these children, except that the vehicles we rode were homemade devices constructed of wood.

We would beg an unneeded wooden milk or soda box from the neighborhood grocer or candy-store proprietor and nail it to a plank. Then we'd fasten roller-skate wheels on the bottom, and add handle bars or steering mechanisms that were nothing more than bits of wood attached to the top of the box at odd angles. Instead of multicolored racing stripes or decals like those decorating these children's vehicles, ours were mostly decorated with bottle caps and pieces of tin or copper. No two scooters were adorned alike; imagination made each scooter unique. Because of this, whenever we happened upon a scooter leaning haphazardly against a pole or carelessly left lying on the ground, we immediately knew who it belonged to.

My scooter's ornamentation was composed of bottle caps hammered at random along the plank, and a flattened piece of tin with a number

7 scratched into it and attached to the front of the box. Another had a plastic Indian nailed to the top of the box and a feather protruding from the rear of the plank. Still another sported pieces of tin cut into different shapes. Whatever the design and however much the scooters lacked beauty and grace, we rode them with pride because we had constructed them ourselves.

Day after day throughout the spring and summer, we lined up side by side along the top of the same hill. We raced to the bottom, pushing the scooters as fast as we could until we reached a designated area, whereupon we jumped onto the plank for the remainder of the downward slope.

We made sounds of police sirens, fire engine bells and racing cars. We always screeched to a halt at the foot of the hill before crossing into the main avenue and traffic. Sometimes we stopped by turning the scooters over onto their sides, stepping quickly out of the way before falling over them. Other times, we spun them around to face the direction from which we had come, leaving scratch marks along the pavement behind us; more simply—and most often—we stopped by banging the scooters broadside against the curb or each other.

Whenever the scooters were damaged, we helped each other carry them home, where we renailed or rescrewed them back into shape. If they were beyond mending, we'd start from scratch with another box, another plank, more bottle caps and tin, and we'd build another so that we could race down that same hill another day. ❖

> *We always screeched to a halt at the foot of the hill before crossing into the main avenue and traffic.*

Facing page: Not all scooters were of the homemade variety. Some young-sters were lucky enough to have a two-wheel, store-bought scooter. Regard-less, scooters of any type were guaranteed to bring hours of enjoyment back in the Good Old Days.

Happy Family Circle!

This "ring-around-the-family" is the happiest hobby in millions of American homes. Father and son (and daughter, too!) team up as engineers of the world's most famous railroad . . . LIONEL! They send those real-life trains highballing around the track with all the extra speed and power of Lionel's exclusive *Magne-Traction*. And it's a joy for Mom, too. She knows everything is running smoothly . . . her family and Lionel Trains.

The big, colorful 1953 Lionel Catalog is great reading for the entire family . . . be sure to drop in at your Lionel dealer's for your copy.

LIONEL TRAINS

Electric Trains

By Bill Brown

A few days ago I had to make one of those dreaded trips up into the attic to empty a water pan that was not draining properly in the air-conditioning box. I dread the trip in the summer because the temperature up there is about 150 degrees.

While I was stumbling around, all stooped over, I came across a box marked "Electric Trains." I had to sit down and open the box. When we lived in a larger house, I could keep both sets up and both trains running through the small town I had created on two large sheets of plywood.

I picked up one of the locomotives and turned it over in my hand. My trains were models of steam locomotives—not the sleek diesels you see today. What memories they conjured up!

When I was a youngster in Canada, my family did all of its traveling on trains. If we went to Montreal to see a hockey game, we rode the train for three hours to get there. If I went with my parents to see my father's parents in Saskatchewan, it was a three-day train ride west across Canada. Then there were trips to visit my mother's folks just outside Detroit—an overnight train ride from our home in Ottawa.

Trains fascinated me, and the joy of traveling on them will never be surpassed by traveling in cars or airplanes, and certainly not by bus. Trains had a character all their own, including passengers, conductors and train crews who went out of their way to be friendly to a little kid.

I vividly remember one trip from western Canada, coming across miles of flat prairie where the Canadian Pacific Railroad tracks ran parallel to those of the Canadian National Railroad. We were traveling on the eastbound CPR train and a CNR train caught up with us. The engineers were racing one another. Everybody on both trains was at the car windows, cheering on their train.

It was exciting—the most excitement I could recall in my young life. My heart was beating fast as I yelled encouragement to our engineer, whom I could not see. Those train whistles were blowing—a great sound I'll never let die.

First our train would edge ahead; then the CNR train would run neck-and-neck with us, before nudging just a little ahead. Our train finally went in front to stay, and as I watched, the CNR train disappeared as its railroad line curled away from ours.

I asked the conductor how fast we were going; I still recall gasping when he told me we must have been going nearly 75 miles per hour. That fireman really had to be shoveling the coal into that firebox. Imagine—75 miles per hour!

Sleeping on a train in a berth is the greatest way to sleep I have ever found. That *clickety-click, clickety-click, clickety-click, clickety-click* never failed to help me nod off in a hurry. And for some reason, eating in the dining car at tables covered with white tablecloths made food taste delicious. To this day I have never eaten trout that was as tasty as the trout they served on a train.

I was telling a friend just yesterday that before I die, I want to travel across the country one more time on a train. It probably won't be the same; nothing ever is the second time around. But maybe—just maybe—using my imagination and my recollections, I can make it come close to being as good as it was back in 1938.

I'm going to try.

And my electric trains? They're coming out of the attic. I'm going to bring them down and set them up again. They deserve to be allowed to run free—and maybe create some good memories for younger people who don't know that trains used to run on coal and wood. ❖

Homemade Toys

By Jay Andrews

Nowadays you seldom if ever see a boy playing with a plaything that he has made himself. Our modern miracle of manufacturing makes everything for him, just as it makes every other needed (and needless) thing. The vast variety of today's ready-made playthings are more attractive, perhaps more durable, and are certainly marvels of mechanical ingenuity; and for these reasons they do have a value. But it occurs to me that they are without that greater worth: the incentive and interest, the pride of prowess, the deep satisfaction that went with contriving a personally made plaything.

Of course, another modern factor that contributes to the abundance of factory-made things, and makes them so readily obtainable, is the affluence that was unknown back in the old days.

Perhaps the most common of old-time playthings was the string ball. Unlike ready-made, hard-rubber varieties and the store-bought balls with stitched covers, the string ball was homemade. And making a good one—one that was firm and well rounded—called for a good deal of patient application and careful workmanship.

The starting point was most important; a fairly round object was needed. A black walnut made a good center, as its reticulated, slightly rough surface kept the first windings in place. From then on the wrappings were laid on with even tension and spacing so that the finished ball would be solid, with a satisfying roundness. The last foot or so of the string was secured by stitching it into the windings.

The games and the uses to which a boy could put a string ball were virtually without limit. There were the games Andy Over, Work-Up, One-Eyed Cat and others. Two boys could play catch, or bat up flies. If no companion was present, a boy could still play catch by himself by flinging the ball up against the gable end of the barn or house and catching it as it bounded back.

He could also bat up flies solo. A short length of board was needed; it was laid across a stick of stove wood and the ball was placed on the lowered end and kept from rolling by a chip. The bat or club was raised and brought down with force on the elevated end of the board. When the blow was true and the board was positioned correctly, the ball would be sent aloft, more or less perpendicularly. The boy then ran and caught it as it came down.

Another item that contributed to a boy's amusement was the throwing stick. In its simplest form it was simply a stick some three feet in length, fairly stiff but with some spring. The tip was pointed for pushing on the harder things. One of the best throwing things to use with the stick was the wild crab. Its hardness held it firmly on the stick so that more force was needed to make it fly off and therefore go farther.

Other things that could be thrown with the sticks were buckeyes, mud balls made from stiff clay and short pieces of corncobs. Old cobs from the pigpen or feedlot were best, as these were moisture-soaked and mud-caked, which made them heavier.

With a piece of string tied to the tip end, the stick could be adapted for throwing a thing like an arrow or a dart made from an inch-wide piece split off a cedar shingle. A couple of inches in from the thin end, the edges of the piece were whittled down to a shaft about the size of a pencil. This reduced air resistance, and the two inches left at the thin end served as a vane. A small slanting notch was cut into the shaft a third of the way back from the butt end.

The thing was thrown by first drawing the knotted end of the string into the notch, holding the vane end with the fingers of one hand and the stick with the other. Then the extended arms were brought back, taking up the slack in the string; then, with a quick twist of the body and a sweep of the stick arm, the thing would be sent into flight. Depending on the intent or whim of the launcher, it would fly aloft or laterally, toward a target or toward nothing at all.

A variation of the throwing stick was the cornstalk-and-horseweed combination. For this, a dry stalk of some four joints was cut and a slot made at the tip end. For projectiles, a patch of dry horseweeds was found. These grew slim and straight to a height of 6 feet or more, and when dry, they were firm and hard. The top end of the weed was positioned in the slot, and the horseweed was held parallel to the cornstalk by the thumb and finger of the hand that grasped the throwing end of the stalk. Propulsion was achieved by bringing the arm and the stalk far back and then sweeping the arm forward, the thumb and finger releasing the weed shaft.

Slingshots were of two kinds, the most common being the one that was made from a forked tree branch, two rubber strips and a pouch made from a piece of leather cut from an old shoe. The other kind of sling was the one that dates back to the time of David and Goliath. This one had a much larger pouch, and with it, stones up to the size of hen's eggs could be thrown. Instead of the rubber strips, two lengths of stout cord or leather thongs were attached to the pouch.

In operation, the end of one cord was looped around the hand and the knotted end of the other cord was held with the thumb and fingers. The pouched stone was then swung in a circle, and when the desired velocity was reached, the knotted end of the cord was released.

The popgun was another homemade plaything that hardly a boy could be completely happy without. This was commonly made from a joint of elderberry with the pith pushed out, and the plunger was a straight, smooth stick that fit loosely in the barrel. Compression was achieved by adding a few windings of string on the forward end of the plunger.

With a small modification that consisted of adding a rubber strip with its ends lashed to the sides of the barrel and the loop end brought back around the end of the plunger (another one that had no string compression), the gun was adapted to fire other kinds of ammunition. These included dried beans and peas, corn kernels, small marbles, pebbles—just about anything that would go into the barrel of the gun.

The hand dart was made from a 2-inch length of corncob, broomstick or other wood of similar size. A slim nail was driven through the length and the protruding end filed sharp. A couple of feathers bound to the body kept the spike end forward when thrown.

Joyful indeed was the fortunate boy who came upon the remaining part of a burned railroad flare on the track. This was a 2-inch length of hardwood or cast iron, about the diameter of a broom handle, and with a spike protruding from the rounded end. Here, come to hand, was a perfectly shaped and proportioned dart, needing only feathers to complete it!

Another game requiring homemade equipment that was enjoyed by the more spirited and adventurous was "bumblebee fighting." The needed equipment was two paddles that could be whittled from almost any kind of board. Armed with these, the intrepid youth would go forth and seek out a bumblebee nest. The game was begun by poking a stick vigorously into the nest and then withdrawing to a suitable distance to await the action—which would be coming forthwith and would be forthright in purpose.

The object of the game lay in the boy's ability to stand his ground and defend himself by smacking with his paddles at the angered bees that came at him. Of course, the paddles were rarely 100-percent effective; even against his most furious efforts, a small few of the belligerent bees would succeed in breaching the ramparts of the flailing paddles and take their vengeance.

But this was just part of the game, and as such, was accepted and suffered. What warrior worthy of the name survives the battlefield without wounds to attest to his valor? ❖

Oh, You Beautiful Doll!

By Dorothy Cole Clayton

When I was a little girl growing up in Massachusetts, boys had the active toys—baseball bats and gloves, hockey sticks, trains, erector sets. All were good, fun toys. Girls were given dolls and, lest they forget their destined role in life, toy irons, pots, pans and sewing kits.

One Christmas, Granny Cole, my father's mother, gave me a boy doll mannequin made of papier-mâché. I think it must have come from Mr. Paul's store on Market Street. The doll was dressed in blue rompers, and wore a cute little beret. The outfit was complete with white shoes and socks. He was cute, but hard to play with, because nothing on him moved. His arms and legs were rigid, as were his neck and head. One day I decided to take him outside to play. Unfortunately, he came to a sorry end when he was dropped and shattered into hundreds of tiny pieces.

The "in" dolls in the 1930s were "doll-in-a-suitcase" dolls. They came in shiny black trunks with golden metal locks. When the trunk was opened, the inside revealed fancy wallpaper. A doll with curly hair stood in the right side of the case, a girl doll dressed in a bathing suit, about 12 inches tall. On the left side was a wooden rod, which held three dresses, and a drawer, which held bedroom slippers and another pair of shoes.

Shirley Temple dolls were usually dressed in red or green polka-dot outfits. The organdy material made waves in her skirt. Shirley was always smiling and looking as though she would burst into *The Good Ship Lollipop*. We can recall her helmet of "baloney curls."

The Alyce Jane McHenry doll represented a 12-year-old girl who needed surgery for an "upside-down stomach." In order to secure money for that unusual and expensive operation, her parents launched a line of clothing and dolls. I remember having a blue dress with a cloth logo of Alyce and the words "I love you" printed on the sleeve.

I envied my friends who possessed any of these dolls. As for me, I never had a doll in a suitcase—no Shirley, and no Alyce Jayne.

Paper dolls—now they were something else indeed. They cost 10 cents a book in Woolworth's. One birthday my mother gave me a 25-cent book of dolls. This book was not filled with the usual prosaic babies and little children. It held pictures of all the first ladies, dressed in the gowns they wore to their husbands'

Shirley Temple doll, 1935 The Household Magazine, House of White Birches nostalgia archives inaugural balls. The costumes illustrated the fashions of the day, from Martha Washington to Eleanor Roosevelt.

These dolls stimulated a latent interest in history and fashion, which has given me much pleasure during my life. I hope my mother realized what a wonderful gift she gave me.

There was another source of paper dolls—Goddard's Department Store in Lynn, Mass. Simplicity and McCall's pattern companies issued a quarterly catalog showing up-to-date fashions. The books were printed on glossy paper, which stood up to hard play when cut out.

Several friends and I would dress up nicely, go into the store and head straight for the pattern counter. We would ask as politely as we knew how, "Do you have any extra pattern books today?" The ladies behind the counter were very genteel and liked pretty manners in girls. They usually found a book for us.

Our bounty secured, we rushed home to cut out the figures and get a game of "house" started. There were many more illustrations of ladies than of men, and quite a few of children's clothes, again, more girls than boys. But I don't remember the lack of males bothering us. We knew where the glamour was!

Imagination knew no bounds. We produced musical shows, singing as we danced the dolls around. Mock weddings caused a bit of trouble because only one doll could be the bride, and it was difficult to decide what the bridesmaids would wear.

When we played "house," we could vent our anger or unhappiness without fear of being rude to a grown-up. That was a good feeling, therapeutic and harmless.

My favorite paper-doll game was "office." I loved being the boss and modeled my dolls after Rosalind Russell or Barbara Stanwyck, high-profile actresses in the 1930s.

Our dolls traveled to Europe, competed in beauty pageants and starred on the stage—all while impeccably dressed. Sometimes we played "hospital," but as two of my friends had vivid memories of having their tonsils removed, that game was not too popular.

All of our make-believe dolls and situations were marvelous developmental tools for us. We didn't realize that at the time, but oh, how we enjoyed playing with them! ❖

Log Cabin Syrup

By Thuma Prichard

Buying syrup used to be an exciting event! It hasn't always come in glass bottles or plastic receptacles. I can remember when Log Cabin Syrup came in a small tin container shaped and painted to look like a log cabin. The cap was the chimney. There were windows and a door, and a bear skin hung against the logs.

There were three of us children at home—my two brothers and me—and we took turns getting the empty log cabins. Chuck was five years older than I, and I fell heir to his share when he became too old to play kid games, but before that time, I used to share in the way he and Bob played pioneer and trapper. The rug was the wilderness with toss-pillow mountains; the bare floor, the rivers and lakes; and the log cabins, our settlement.

Matches used to come in pasteboard boxes. As soon as they were empty, we stacked them, pasted them together and they became barns, stores and other buildings.

We transformed them into covered wagons and supply carts, too, making complicated harnesses and reins for the clothespin horses to pull them. On Mondays (didn't everyone wash on Monday?), Mother stood, hands on hips, and demanded the return of the entire herd, impatiently waiting while we undid the intricate string tack. Sometimes we'd have as many as six horses in a hitch.

My imaginary heroine rode ahead of the wagon train over the sofa-mountain on a clothespin steed Mother let me crayon black. It was given a special dispensation from the Monday clothesline.

Cardboard was always in demand and we saved the backs of our Big Chief school tablets. Carefully drawing around the bottom of the salt shaker (it was exactly the right size), we fashioned cardboard wheels and attached them to our rolling stock with straight pins.

I remember trying to be fancy and cutting out spokes, but it weakened the wheels so much that they collapsed under the load we put in our wagons. So I went back to drawing in the spokes.

Chuck and Bob had deadly battles with Indians and "bad men," but I preferred making and stocking a little homestead with my log cabins, tiny cardboard tables, benches and cradles.

Lynn Peters (my favorite name for all my heroines) would fall in love with an Indian chief, much to the scoffing of my two brothers. They kept racing their wagons across the rug plateaus and bare-floor rivers, chasing Indians just when Lynn wanted to settle down with her handsome chief.

That was all over a half-century ago. I suppose it speaks well for Log Cabin Syrup to still be around, but with the disappearance of the little log cabins, a whole land of make-believe was lost. ❖

The Gift

By Lee D. Pirolozzi Sr.

School was out for the summer. I was an 8-year-old boy dressed in patched knickerbockers—not uncommon for that time. My home was a tarpaper shack built in a field, 200 or 300 yards from the main road, and I lived there with my mother and father. We were dirt poor, without electricity, running water or inside plumbing. But even without these "necessities," I was healthy, clean and happy, and ready to take on another bright summer day.

My plans were formulated when I saw a bunch of my friends mounted on bicycles loaded down with bats, balls and gloves; obviously they were headed for the ball field. I called to my mother, telling her that I was leaving and ran across the field at full speed. But the boys on the bicycles didn't see me, and the gap between them and me widened rapidly. It was times like this that I wished I had a bicycle, but I knew that it was not to be.

The old man on the porch of the house nearby had watched this scenario many times, but today he shouted, "Come here, boy!" I stopped to see who had called me. The old gentleman repeated his summons.

The house, which sat 100 feet or so from the road, had a porch that ran the full width of the front. Its weather-beaten railing with several missing rungs was broken at the one corner. The man sat on an ancient wooden rocking chair, smoking a corncob pipe. An aged coonhound with bloodshot eyes watched as I approached the house.

Stopping at the bottom of the steps, I was silent and respectful, as I had been taught, and I waited for the man to speak. The antiquated chair protested loudly as the old man leaned forward to get a better look at me.

I was curious. Why had I been called today?

I had seen the old man and his dog around town and sitting on his porch, as today, smoking his corncob pipe, but I had never paid attention to them. But now here I stood, at the bottom of the porch steps, looking up into a ruddy, lined face, a face weathered by many years of hard work.

"Don't have a bicycle, do you, boy?"

"No, Sir."

The old man carefully laid his pipe down on the porch beside his chair. He reached down and scratched the hound's ears, then got up. "Come on, Joshua, let's go see if we can help this young man."

I was surprised at how tall the man was when he stood up. I followed him as he went around the corner of the porch and headed for the huge, white bank barn. Joshua followed, sniffing at my heels.

Two large doors hanging from rusted rails were wedged shut by long logs leaning halfway up on each door. The old man removed one log and slid the barn door open. The squeaking rollers brought forth a flurry of screeching and squawking and a cascade of feathers and dust as the pigeons inside scurried for safety. Sunshine streamed in through the cracks between the wide boards, exaggerating the falling dust.

The barn had not lost all of its flavor, even though it had not housed livestock for many years. The pungent odor of old straw and hay mingled with the scent left behind by horses and cows. Only one part of the cavernous building was still used for storage—the area where hay had been stored when this was a working farm.

While we waited for the dust to settle, I studied the massive, hand-hewn beams that framed the structure. I was awestruck by the building's size; it didn't look so big from the road. A wooden snatch block hung from a crossbeam, high over the main floor. A rope threaded through it was tied to a rail below. Alongside a

Playing Cowboy by Amos Sewell © 1951 SEPS: Licensed by Curtis Publishing

primitive hay baler, a wooden fanning mill balanced itself on its three remaining legs.

The old gentleman pointed to a pile of farm tools stacked against the wall; they were covered with dust, pigeon droppings and spider webs. Among the hodgepodge, I could see the frame of a bicycle. The black paint had been chipped and scratched, and the handlebars were rusted.

"Dig it out and it's yours," the farmer said with a smile.

With the old coonhound sniffing at every implement, I carefully played "pickup stix" with an array of forks, rakes and shovels. I finally extracted my prize and put everything back.

It was a 28-inch bicycle with wooden wheel rims and two flat tires that were badly checked by years of storage and neglect. There was no way I could ever hope to replace them. The old man saw the look of despair on my face. Without saying anything, he started to look around the barn as I watched with interest. Finally the old man found a coil of garden hose hanging on a peg and brought it to where the bicycle lay.

The pneumatic tires were tubeless, and shellacked to the rim. The method for repairing flats was the same back then as it is today: forcing a piece of rubber coated with rubber cement into the hole in the tire with a long, needlelike instrument. After the "fix" was allowed to dry, the tire was pumped full of air.

I watched inquisitively as my fairy godfather turned the bicycle over and rested it on its seat and handlebars. Then he reached into his overalls for his pocketknife, and cut each tire, taking great care not to cut too far. When he was satisfied that he had cut each tire about halfway through, he squared the end of the hose and inserted it into the tire and forced it around until the end showed up again at the origin. Then he cut the hose and forced the split end around the inside of the tire until it was opposite the cut. He repeated the process on the other tire.

His sweat was now dripping onto the floor,

The grin on my face was all the thanks the old man needed. Many years ago, another child had grinned his gratitude at his father … but that was long ago.

but the old man found an oilcan and oiled the pedals, chain and bearings. He turned the rear wheel with the pedals and when he applied the coaster brake, the wheel squealed to a stop. Then he straightened himself up and wiped his face with a huge blue handkerchief.

"Well, boy, can you ride?"

"Yes, Sir."

Turning the vehicle onto its wheels, he pushed it toward me. "Let's see you ride it up and down the driveway."

As I put the mounting pedal up, the man's mind raced back to another little boy who had done the same thing, a long time ago, when the bicycle was new, its shining frame reflecting the sun. He smiled with the deep satisfaction of knowing that he had made two little boys happy.

The grin on my face was all the thanks the old man needed. Many years ago, another child had grinned his gratitude at his father … but that was long ago, before influenza had taken him away.

I thanked the man, but it wasn't necessary. The gift was indeed from the heart, a truly precious gift.

I didn't find out about the man's son and the bicycle until many years later.

I always stopped at the old farmer's house whenever I saw him sitting on the porch. One day I thought I saw him in the backyard and I stopped, but it was somebody else. The man told me that Mr. Johnson had gone away. I found out later that he had died.

I hope he wasn't looking down the day Bill and I were riding double. With Bill at the controls, we crossed the railroad tracks and rolled down the embankment onto the highway into the path of an oncoming automobile. Bill was scraped up a little and I got a sprained ankle. But the bicycle was damaged beyond repair.

Wherever you are, Mr. Johnson, thanks for two great years of bicycling—and for making a young fellow's wish come true, way back there in the Good Old Days. ❖

Childhood Swings

By Misty Talcott

I suspect that the swing's evolution had something to do with the great desire of all wingless creatures to fly.

I'm sure there has never lived a child who has not envied a bird its wings or who has not, at one time or another, been a king in a swing, flying back and forth, exulting in the heady heights, and surveying his kingdom from the apex of its arch.

But when you reach middle life, swings become nostalgia. And what memories they can evoke—from the grapevine swing at the old swimming hole to the glittering, glimmering, whirl-you-away contraptions you loved at the county fair.

It's true that there are swings made of chain, of rope and of cable. There are board seats, tire seats and hobos. But whatever they are made of, they all let you fly through the air without wings.

When I was a child, I always had a swing. Mine was not a backyard contrivance bought at a store, but a real swing, fastened high on a tree limb, that really let me fly.

My mother used to push me when I was small, and sometimes I would go higher than she was tall. From way up there, I would look down on her head and, for one short moment, I didn't feel small at all.

When I was older, I'd swing by myself. I'd pump up high, leaning with the wind and pushing with the momentum, until my head flew even with the limb. Then, with my bottom secure on the old board seat, I'd soar with eagles, race with the seagulls and fly with the girl on the circus trapeze. After all these years, I still say that airplanes, jets, helicopters and such things have no thrill like that offered by the old board swing.

Yes, I was a swinger. My mother used to say that if you wanted to know my whereabouts, just listen for the squeak of a swing.

For rainy days and those "don't get your clothes dirty" times, there was always the front porch swing. Mama would get me dressed for a special occasion and say, "Don't get dirty now. Go swing until I'm ready."

I remember long summer days in the old porch swing, with Rag Doll secured by her apron strings, with Kitten in my lap and Puppy beside me (baby ducklings and chicks never liked swings, I guess, because they had their own wings). We could glide to and fro and I'd sing them a song, until a yap or a meow betrayed us.

Then my mother would call, "Are you swinging animals again?"

"Yes, Ma'am."

Then she'd always say, "Just you be careful they don't fall and get hurt."

"Yes, Ma'am."

After that, I'd give a hard kick and Dolly would nod, the swing would groan, and away we would go to a magical land, where I was queen and animals talked and grown-ups were never allowed. Oh, those were the good days—the golden days of my childhood—when imagination was free and fantasies were all so real.

My mama's most cherished photograph was in a frame on the head of her bed. I found it last year when I went through her things, buried deep in a box marked "Keep." It was a picture of Kitten, Puppy and me, fast asleep in that old porch swing. On the back she had written in her scrawling hand, "My little girl and her animals asleep on the swing—June 1933."

Yes, the sight of a swing is the magic carpet of my middle years. It can whisk me away to that wonderful place where only memory can go, to the days of kittens and puppies, and dollies and ducklings—and the little girl who was queen in the old porch swing. ❖

Children on Swing by Eugene Iverd © 1935 SEPS: Licensed by Curtis Publishing

Now *That's* Entertainment

Chapter Five

I know today's younger set think they have a corner on the market of entertainment. Movie houses now have 12 and more theatres housed in a single multiplex. Most homes have either cable or satellite television with dozens—if not hundreds—of channels. The television in many homes now is a high definition set and, with a surround sound system, rivals many movie theatres. There are also dozens of radio stations offering every type of music imaginable.

But entertainment back in the Good Old Days was so fresh with new ideas and possibilities, even if it was rather rough around the edges. Can you imagine what it was like when the "flickers"—as movies were called way back then—added sound? What about the first time a radio station from faraway cities was amplified instead of coming over earphones via a crystal radio set? Television was fuzzier than an alpaca jacket when it first made its way into our homes, but it still had a magical quality—*live* moving pictures.

I think when you compare entertainment today with that of yesteryear, there was something else that really set it apart, however. It was the *humanity*.

Yes, there was some escapism in going to the movies, but the movie theatre was where we went to be *with* other people, not get away from them. Now we can wait a few months after a movie leaves the big screen and it is on one of the television movie channels. But part of the entertainment was the journey when you were a farm kid and you didn't get to town all that often. Part of it was getting together with the gang and seeing a Tom Mix western, not to mention a cliffhanger serial and a cartoon. Part of it was the popcorn or candy during the movie, or the ice cream cone at the drug store soda fountain afterwards.

Now as you drive through block after block of houses in suburbia, you will see the flicker of televisions in almost every home. Inside, there might even be other televisions, video games or computers in other rooms as the humanity is divided even more.

In the Good Old Days, we pretended we were making our own movies or plays in the back yard on summer evenings with our best friends. At fair time the same group and their families shared time at the carnival. At card parties, the old Philco radio added music or comedy to the evening, but the emphasis was the fun we were having *together*.

More isn't always better. We had less of everything—less movies, less music, less radio and almost no television. But what we had gave us more thrills than a dozen multiplexes, and left us exclaiming: "Now *that's* entertainment!"

—*Ken Tate*

When the Circus Came To Town

By Angie Monnens

With the end of another school term, my brothers, sisters and I looked forward to a fun-filled summer—baseball games in the park, swimming in the river near the dam and picnics on Lookout Point. We spent happy hours on treks in the woods picking wildflowers, or just watching the squirrels and rabbits playing hide-and-seek. Tap dancing and orchestra practice kept us busy, too. Occasional visits to our uncle's farm made time pass quickly in Cold Spring, Minn., where I grew up back in the 1930s.

But on a hot August night in 1933, the circus came to town, and I have never forgotten it. I had never seen a circus before, and the anticipation made my heart pound. As huge trucks and vans rolled down the road, everyone gathered around to welcome them. Even the town band closed up shop for a while and accompanied the trucks as they made their way to the park to camp for the night.

As huge trucks and vans rolled down the road, everyone gathered around to welcome them. Even the town band closed up shop for a while and accompanied the trucks as they made their way to the park to camp for the night.

With bated breath we waited for them to uncover all the mysterious things inside the massive vehicles and trailers. As the unloading began, a great hulk of a man with a long, flowing beard and scraggly black hair approached. In a gruff, booming voice, he said, "If I let you kids watch, it will spoil all the surprises when the big tent opens tonight. Go home, kiddies, but be sure to come back tonight!"

Disappointed, we reluctantly headed home to wait as patiently as possible until 7 o'clock. I could not tell time yet, so I pestered Mama every few minutes. "What time is it now, Mama? Almost time to go?"

"Not now," she answered. "I will let you know. As soon as supper is over and you are all dressed up, it will be time to go."

When the magic moment arrived we dressed in our best clothes

and Sunday patent-leather shoes. Mama handed us our money tied in a knot in the corner of Daddy's white handkerchief. All the way uptown, we checked our pockets to make sure the money was still there, safe and sound.

Mama's words rang in my ears all the way: "Now don't lose your money, yah hear now?" So I kept my hands in my pockets as we neared the lot.

Long lines of bright lights had transformed the lot into a buzzing, bustling square. It was a jumble of tents, booths and stands, and masses of people milled around. The delicious aromas of greasy hamburgers, grilled hot dogs, fresh taffy and buttered popcorn filled the air.

The focal point, a huge gray tent, was surrounded by tables crammed with goodies— Kewpie dolls with sassy eyes and protruding tummies, stuffed animals, and games of skill. Handmade beads in every color caught my eye; I had never seen anything so beautiful in my entire life.

We shoved and pushed our way to the big top, and after paying a dime, we were allowed inside. The heat under the tent was so intense that I could barely breathe. The smell of sweaty bodies mingled with the sawdust and the stench of animals. The odor was overwhelming so I threw the rest of my hamburger behind the seats as we climbed to the very top row.

Accompanied by a steady roll of drums, the ringmaster entered, dressed in a bright red spangled suit, black top hat and gloves, to announce the start of the show. In amazement we watched the trapeze artists in their skin-tight, silver-and-green costumes literally fly through the air!

There were dancing bears, clowns tumbling and rolling among the crowd, elephants performing impossible tricks and prancing ponies. Lions roared ferociously as they waited in golden cages to entertain the spectators.

Hours passed quickly and soon it was time to go home. But we didn't want to miss a thing,

so we wandered from trailer to tent, trying to decide which one to see. Our last dime would have to give us something very special to be remembered for a long time. Strolling nearby we heard the bellowing chant of the barker above the noisy crowds.

"Hahry, hah-h-h-ry, get your tickets now! Don't delay! You don't want to miss this for all the money in the world! Inside you'll be transported to a mysterious land—the closest thing to paradise you'll ever see!"

As the people began to line up, we hastily decided that this *surely* must be well worth our last dime. It was unanimous, so we entered, found a bench and waited. The curtain parted—and there stood 12 young women with dark black hair, all very scantily clad. They performed an unfamiliar dance, which I was sure Mama would have called sinful. Their hips swayed back and forth in time to the music like the pendulum on Grandpa's wooden clock.

As they continued their dance, my brothers hooted and hollered, as did other males in the audience. We girls, however, were most uncomfortable. I felt my cheeks blush with shame; I couldn't wait till it ended.

We girls left in a hurry, dragging our brothers along. On the way home we made a secret pact never to divulge to Mama what we had seen. With my heart filled to bursting with excitement and my tummy bursting with the food I had consumed, I went to bed dreaming of all I had seen.

It was an occasion I have never forgotten—a mystical, magical night when a dreary, empty corner lot became a noisy, exciting fairyland. ❖

Carnival Time

By Cathy Taylor

Once upon a time, kids had fun without electric gadgets, high-tech toys or gobs of money. We exercised our imagination and played "pretend" games. Boys with only an old cowboy hat and a broomstick horse played cowboys and rustlers with arguments as to who would be which. No one wanted to be the bad guy—they all wanted to be Ken Maynard with his horse, Tarzan. Girls played movie star with Mom's old dresses and high heels. My favorite star was tap dancer Ruby Keeler.

When I wasn't pretending, I was dreaming about joining a carnival. I didn't know what I'd do there, but I was enchanted by the bright lights, laughing people, merry-go-round calliope music and the excitement of that strange world. To me it seemed like the Emerald City.

The carnival came for our county fair and I got to go once or twice each year. Dad knew the owner of the carnival; he called him a "carny." I thought this man was wonderful because he gave me "ducats." That was his name for tickets to get into the shows and ride the rides free. When I got ducats, I was the envy of the neighborhood kids. But I wondered, *If I joined the carnival, couldn't I ride free all the time?*

The crowds especially seemed to like the hootchy-kootchy dancers with their gold bangles and tambourines.

Even before we reached the midway, I smelled frying hamburgers and onions. Even today, I've not yet found another place where I can capture that same tantalizing aroma and sizzle that said, "Carnival!" The hamburgers were not complete without Orange Crush and shoestring potatoes—and all for 25 cents. If I had a spare quarter, that's where it went.

But if I didn't get ducats, I didn't eat. I kept my money for the rides. At a dime a ride, my precious stash, which I'd struggled to save, would last for most of what I wanted to do. And I had to save a dime for my annual souvenir: four pictures on a strip.

The midway was paved with sawdust, dirt and beaten-down grass. On rainy days it turned into a muddy mess, but we went anyway. The rides were set up along the center of the midway, and strung out on both sides were the games and shows. The games posed an array of challenges. I was never very good, but I tried. I liked the pitch-till-you-win because I always got some trinket, like a tiny celluloid Kewpie doll. It wasn't worth the dime it cost, but it was exciting—and at least it was a prize. I watched men wind up and try to pitch a baseball to knock over white wooden milk bottles, and try to shoot little yellow tin ducks running along a track. The winners

received a stuffed animal or a gaudy plaster-of-paris figurine.

Punctuating the noise were the singsong voices of the barkers, trying to coax people in to see the shows. "Hey there, Mister, come on in! Bring your sweetie!" Mom wouldn't let me go in to watch most of the shows. I could only watch the performers who came out on the stage.

The crowds especially seemed to like the hootchy-kootchy dancers with their gold bangles and tambourines. Mom made me cover my eyes—but I peeked. The girls, dressed in bright, filmy skirts and veils, shimmied their hips to the music.

Once we saw a family troupe of Hawaiians. To me they looked like they were from a foreign land. I was intrigued by the ladies in leis and grass skirts as they danced to their own music. *If I joined the carnival, I bet I could do that,* I thought. I wondered what they wore in the winter.

The rides, of course, were the most fun. The merry-go-round was tame, even when I managed to get one of the glittering, moving horses with big glass eyes and bared teeth. The spinning, cup-shaped Tilt-A-Whirl and the swinging Chair-O-Plane made me dizzy and everyone screamed, but we all loved it. And although it was tamer, I liked the rolling up-and-down caterpillar with its green, tentlike cover.

But the Ferris wheel was my very favorite. From the top I could see the whole fairgrounds—the grandstand, the rodeo chutes and the animal barns at the back. When the seat swayed, I clutched the crossbar more tightly. The tingling excitement left me shaky.

Once I strayed away from my folks and then wandered around by myself, taking in the fascinating sights. Mom was awfully angry when they finally found me. "Now listen here, young lady," she warned me. "You stick with me or you'll never come here again!" That did it. I behaved. *But I could go wherever I wanted if I joined the carnival, couldn't I?*

When I was 10 years old, my friend Ruthie and I were allowed to go to the carnival without our parents, providing we stuck close to her 16-year-old sister, Velma. But Velma had a boyfriend and didn't want two little kids tagging along. We had ridden most of the rides except the Ferris wheel and we begged to go on that, too. Strangely, not only did Velma agree to let us go while she waited, but she even offered to buy the tickets. Gee whiz, wasn't that great?

Ruthie and I giggled with delight as we rode up and down, around and around. But it soon dawned on us that the ride seemed longer than usual. When the wheel finally slowed and then stopped to let us off, we told the man running it that the ride had been a really long one. He laughed. "The girl who bought your tickets gave me enough for two rides each."

Velma and her boyfriend were nowhere around. Naturally, we didn't look too hard for them.

After awhile, Velma found us. She said that we had better not tell her mom or my mom about the extra ride on the Ferris wheel or she would say that we had strayed away and gotten lost.

Velma's threat--and the double ride—bought my silence. I didn't want anything to hurt my chances of returning to the carnival mideway, my yellow brick road to a magical land back in the Good Old Days. ❖

I was intrigued by this Hawaiian troupe that performed at the carnival when I was a child.

Carousel Time by Charles Berger, House of White Birches nostalgia archives

Depression Entertainment

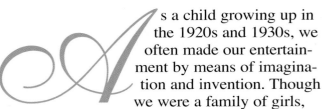

By Irene Dunn

As a child growing up in the 1920s and 1930s, we often made our entertainment by means of imagination and invention. Though we were a family of girls, we sometimes made stilts to walk on and even fixed the stick to roll a hoop.

Another of our fun toys was the can-and-string telephone. We could set up housekeeping with our sleepy-eye dolls and the clothes Grandma had sewn for them. Perhaps one of us established a home by the lilacs, another under an elm tree across the yard. We would call our neighbor on the can phone.

It was fun making ballet dancers of hollyhock flowers. We would line them up on boxes and pretend we had a store full of many-colored ballerina dolls for sale.

Sometimes our store would sell soda fizzes made with vinegar, soda and water. They were fun to make, but really not too good to drink. But we loved mixing them to see them fizz until Mom put a stop to our using her soda and vinegar.

In winter we used the old Sears catalog and cut out the prettiest heads and clothes and made paper dolls. Our dolls could have many, many outfits. None of the store paper dolls had as many clothes as ours, and when they wore out from hard play, we just picked another head and more outfits.

One of my best gifts was when my grandpa bought us girls clamp-on ball-bearing roller skates. We wore the key to turn the clamps on a string around our neck.

We lived in town where there were cement sidewalks, which were ideal for skating. On Saturday, Mother would let us go to the courthouse square, where there was lots of cement, and we'd skate for hours.

I remember many falls that took the knees out of my long stockings. Mother would darn them. I hated darned stockings until one of my teachers told me my mother did the neatest darning she had ever seen. From then on I was proud of my stockings with Mother's small, smooth, neat stitches.

The library was close to the courthouse and the librarian was a sweet lady, friendly and helpful to all of us children. Each of us girls finally had our own library card; I remember the day I got mine.

It was special, for now I could get a book by myself without Mother. We loved to read, and I remember that each Saturday, after our usual chores were finished, we would return books to the library and skate awhile. On our way home we would stop at the library and browse for a book to take home to read.

I loved going down the shelf of the *Bobbsey Twins* and the *Twins of the World;* I read them all. Next it was Thornton Burgess books and the *Five Little Peppers* family.

From these we went to Louisa May Alcott, Frances Hodgeson Burnett, Edna Ferber and eventually Faith Baldwin, Bess Streeter Aldrich, Kathleen Norris and many more in the adult section. Mother got magazines at the library to read instead of subscribing, like people do today.

I still love to read, and fear many have lost much pleasure by turning to television. How great to be able to choose when, what and where we want adventure by reading at our leisure!

Another of our joys was going downtown on Saturday nights. All the farmers and their families came to purchase groceries and supplies for the following week. It was fun to meet friends and attend concerts on the courthouse lawn. I loved to be there when the band was setting up in the bandstand and listen as they tuned their instruments. I still love band music, and I think that those Saturday-night concerts I enjoyed while growing up helped me acquire my love for it.

Many times, on our way to the courthouse lawn, we would smell

Bandstand Entertainment by Charles Berger, House of White Birches nostalgia archives

fresh buttered popcorn. Then we knew that Mr. Bailey's popcorn wagon was parked on the street nearby. We purchased some to eat during the band concert.

He was always near the theater when it was movie time, too. I loved to have him pour hot butter from his coffeepot over my bag of popcorn. After the movie we often went to Livingston's Café to get a 5-cent hamburger.

Sometimes after attending the Saturday matinee at the theater we would go to the corner drugstore fountain and have a "sleigh ride." That was Mr. Wanek's name for an ice-cream soda. They came in many flavors, and we loved to sit at the round table with the wire-back chairs and enjoy our goodies.

One summer the drugstores had an ice-cream war. We could buy a quart for 10 cents! We kids would go in, get a quart, have them cut it in two and give us two little wooden spoons. Off we would go and gorge ourselves until we were nearly sick. But it wouldn't be many days before we were back for another flavor.

Another business of Mr. Bailey's was the miniature golf course. We loved taking some of our 10-cents-an-hour baby-sitting money to play a round of golf on his course. Again, his wagon was there for after-game snacks.

Our Depression toys and entertainment provided us with lots of pleasure because we were imaginative and inventive as we created our fun. We were happy children and didn't realize what we didn't have, for most of our friends lived in much the same manner. ❖

After the Movie by Stevan Dohanos © 1947 SEPS: Licensed by Curtis Publishing

Saturday Matinees

By Robert R. Law

The Saturday-afternoon movie was a big event in our lives back in the 1930s. All week we discussed and argued about how the hero in the current serial would escape the certain doom that faced him when he was last seen, hanging over the cliff on a frayed rope that the villain was gleefully cutting! Our curiosity would be satisfied the following week, but then we would be left with another enigma. "Now, I ask you, how could he avoid being blown to bits? He was sitting right on top of the dynamite!" And so it went, week after week.

It only cost a dime to go to the movies on Saturday. Sometimes we received a free candy bar or comic book with admission. What a bargain—two movies, cartoons and a serial, all for 10 cents!

The movies we liked most were westerns that featured stars like Gene Autry and Hopalong Cassidy. We loved the way Hopalong would mosey up to the bar, put his boot on the brass rail, tip back his hat and order a sarsaparilla. No rotgut or red-eye for him. We thought that was really keen.

It only cost a dime to go to the movies on Saturday. Sometimes we received a free candy bar or comic book with admission.

There were no shades of gray in those days; there were the good guys and the bad guys and that was it. The good guys wore white hats and the bad guys wore black hats. The same went for their horses, whose colors matched the hats. The good guys always toted a pair of shiny silver six-shooters with pearl handles, and oh, how we dreamed of owning a set just like them! Needless to say, the bad guys always carried plain, dark metal handguns.

Inevitably, near the end of the movie, the bad guys would take off with their ill-gotten loot, only to be cut off at the pass by the good guys. I often wondered why the bad guys never knew about the shortcut.

There was always a pretty girl involved, and the hero would smile at her now and then, but there was none of that sloppy kissin' stuff, thank goodness. We all knew that he had a much better relationship with his horse anyway!

We also had Tarzan and Flash Gordon movies and serials starring Buster Crabbe and Johnny Weismuller, and comedians like Charlie Chaplin and Laurel and Hardy, who made us laugh until we hurt.

We never saw adults at the Saturday matinee, and small wonder, for it was bedlam. Everybody arrived early in order to get a good seat. The best ones, we thought, were in the very front row. So we had a half-hour or more to have fun before the show started. I couldn't hear myself think with hundreds of kids yelling and shouting.

First we had to check out what kind of candy everybody had, and if it was more appealing than what we had, we tried to trade: "I'll give you half of my candy bar if you give me half of yours. Hey! Your half is smaller than the half I gave you!"

Kids scooted out of their seats and ran to the lobby for additional sweets, or ran to greet others they knew. There was a lot of hat throwing, causing their owners to climb or crawl under seats to retrieve them. Numerous confrontations arose from the disturbing, uncomfortable presence of feet pushing in the back of one's seat.

Once the lights dimmed, however, there would come a great roar of approval. The horseplay would cease and the noise would spiral down to a whisper as the big screen transported us into a world of fantasy.

During the week, we became the hero of the hottest movie or current serial. I remember how we tied lengths of clothesline to the end of a stick to make whips when we became Zorro.

A black paper mask completed the transformation. The mask was also great for becoming the Lone Ranger, and so our play imitations came and went, from serial to serial.

Frequently, we did not have the price of admission. In these sorry circumstances, we made up devious schemes to sneak in. A simple but dangerous way was to have a friend who paid for his admission go down the outside aisle and open one of the fire exit doors. His poverty-stricken buddies, who were waiting outside, would rush in and scatter throughout the theater.

The problem with this method was that once the doors were opened, the theater was flooded with bright outdoor light, instantly alerting the ushers to the skullduggery. They would come running down the aisles and apprehend anyone they could catch. So the success rate of this method was about fifty-fifty; too risky for my taste.

Then one of my friends discovered where the theater threw out all the used ticket stubs. We never could find two that matched, however, because the theater patron always kept one half! A few kids tried gluing two stubs together anyway, and without a close inspection, the ticket appeared to be genuine. However, they soon discovered with sickening hearts that the theater frequently changed the color of the tickets. Hey, the life of crime is not easy, "the Shadow knows …"

Then there was the walk-in-backwards trick. We waited until the first showing was over and the crowd began to exit the theater. Then we'd slowly walk in backward against the flow of exiting people.

We'd keep an eye out for the usher, and if we saw one, we'd walk ahead a little bit, just as if we too were on our way out. Then, when he was distracted, we continued our backward movement until we were inside. This took nerve and skill and was not recommended for the tender-hearted.

Our life of crime came to an end when we were hired to distribute advertising handbills for the theater. Our pay was free admission! Also, some of us became paper boys, and with the 50- or 60-cent profit at the end of the week, the world was ours.

There was no Disneyland or television in those days. The movies were our great escape. I always got a headache when I emerged from the darkened theater into the bright sunlight. But watching movies for four or five hours was considered normal. Sometimes we would stay and watch the whole thing over again! In fact, I remember getting a little groggy after my long movie watch, and it took some time to get back to reality.

One time, Ivor, the youngest of the three Foley boys, was absent from the Foley supper table. We all remembered that he had been with us at the movies, but we couldn't recall him coming home with us. That night, Mrs. Foley went to the closed theater where she was lucky enough to find the manager locking up and on his way out. He assured her that the theater was empty, but after she pleaded for one more look, the manager consented. With a flashlight in hand, they found Ivor. He was curled up, sound asleep, in the front row—right where we had left him.

The old Palace Theater in Troy, N.Y., has long since been torn down, along with thousands of others throughout the country. But the mystique of these fun-filled castles will always have a special place in the hearts of all those who grew up with them. ❖

Lights Out! Camera! Action!

By Rod C. Peabody

Is anybody out there old enough to remember the "home movies" of the 1920s and 1930s? They were shown on real projectors just like the ones the theaters used, only smaller. They had a hand crank on the right side and mechanisms for holding the full reel on top and the empty reel below the projector.

For Christmas my folks would get me one or two "big" presents and a lot of smaller ones like socks or shoes, all practical stuff. Well, in 1927, to my surprise, I got an erector set *and* one of these new home movie cameras. It was a real shock; I thought I didn't have a chance for a projector, but there it was on Christmas morning under the tree!

Dad had it assembled, and as soon as I could open my other presents, including the large erector set, I pleaded with Mom to hang an old sheet on the basement wall so I could try it out. The whole family wanted to see it work. So Mom hung the sheet while Dad and I set up the projector.

I had the instructions memorized already, including the one about burning yourself on the 150-watt bulb. Of course, that happened several times anyway.

Finally we were ready. The folks and my sister Janice were sitting on boxes and crates. I flipped the lights off and the projector on and started cranking. I will never forget what came on the white sheet screen! It was *The Days of Old, The Days of Gold, The Days of '49*. It was a Western about the gold rush in California and that's all I can remember. There was one big reel that lasted about half an hour.

The projector flickered a little and took some practice to crank the handle smoothly, but it really was a pretty good picture.

I believe Dad got it from Montgomery Ward, and they had a real neat rental system so you didn't have to buy the films. We sent in the old reel, and for about 50 cents, they sent any one of a couple hundred they had available. You could keep them a month, I think, and then they had to be returned, with or without the 50 cents.

You can guess what happened in the neighborhood. The Peabodys and their ornery kid, Rod, became very popular. Mom, bless her heart, would make popcorn and lemonade for all the kids to enjoy while watching "the movie." They would even chip in a nickel or dime to get a new movie, and that helped expenses a lot. We got to see new pictures about every week.

For a couple of years or so, we had regular movie nights (Mom's orders). Ten or more kids would gather at our house on movie night. Their moms helped out by sending apples, oranges, cookies and stuff with their kids.

Westerns were the most popular, but we saw others, too. Charlie Chaplin, Joe E. Brown, and Wheeler and Woolsey jump to my mind. Tom Mix was number one, of course. I imagine that we saw a lot of actors and actresses who later became stars in the "talkies," but my steel-trap mind is rusty and forgetful. I can't recall any names except the big ones.

In fact, I can't recall whatever happened to that Jim-dandy moving-picture machine, or the erector set … or the electric train I bought myself, or my tricycle, or pedal automobile, or scooter, or Daisy pump gun, or ice skates, or model airplane, or … . Whatever happened to all those things you were so proud of at age eight or nine? I guess they just fade away with your childhood. ❖

My First Movie

By Paula Wells

The year was 1934 and I was 10 years old. I couldn't believe my ears when Mom said, "Well, kids, tomorrow is payday, and if Uncle Sam sends us our pension check, we'll go to town on Saturday to a motion picture. How would you like that?"

Like it? I was dumbfounded. I had never seen a movie, and it was the first "talkie" that my mother would see. Entertainment was sparse in those days. We did not even have a radio. We lived in an isolated hollow in Kentucky. It was not often that we got to town to shop, much less see a movie.

Mom drove us three kids to the nearby town of Portsmouth in Southern Ohio. We crossed the Grant Bridge over the broad Ohio River and parked down Gallia Street near the theater. Our B-Model Ford sped us over the winding gravel road at 35 to 40 miles per hour. I thought that fast in those days.

After a lengthy wait in line that Saturday afternoon, we reached the ticket window. Mom purchased all four tickets for less than a dollar. When we reached the lobby, the usher came with a flashlight to show us to our seats. The movie house was packed. My eyes adjusted to the darkness. After the newsreel and cartoon, the movie began.

The movie was *Treasure Island*. I soon became entranced by the magic world I saw on the screen. In my imagination, I became the cabin boy, Jim Hawkins (played by Jackie Cooper), and sailed the ocean with Dr. Livesey to hunt treasure. Jim hid in the apple barrel and heard one-legged Captain Silver (Wallace Beery) plot with the pirates to steal the treasure for themselves. On the island, Jim helped defend the stockade against pirate attack. He climbed the ship's mast to escape the pirate who came after him with a dagger between his teeth.

In the end, I did not think that Jim should have helped the wily Captain Silver escape after all the bad things he had done. But Jim had come under the spell of Silver's (and Wallace Beery's) charm and smooth tongue.

Mom poked me in the ribs and said, "Get up. The movie's finished." I reluctantly awoke from my dazed state and left the theater. Outside, on the streets of Portsmouth, I was shocked to find myself in the real world again, without pirates or treasure chests.

After we got home, we played Treasure Island all that summer vacation. We took turns being the different characters, shooting imaginary muskets at each other. "Ker-pow, you're dead, Long John Silver!" we shouted.

When I saw my second movie the next year, I was almost as fascinated as before. This movie was *The Littlest Rebel* with curly-haired, dimpled Shirley Temple dressed in Civil War costume. As battles swirled around her, she had the great dancer Bill Robinson as her protector.

I sat on the edge of my seat when the Yankees came to her house and Shirley hid her father, a Rebel soldier, in the attic. I despaired when the Yankees later caught him and sentenced him to hang. Would Shirley be able to save her father? Since my own father was dead, this question was especially heart-rending.

By the time Shirley and Bill Robinson had tap-danced their way to Washington, D.C., to see Mr. Lincoln and obtain a pardon for her father, I was lost in a dream world. Then the theater lights came on. When I walked out into the plain streets of Portsmouth, I half-expected to see a tiny blond waif dancing with a tall black man for pennies at the street corner.

Though that was over 70 years ago, my first movies will remain in my memories forever. ❖

Facing page: American child actress, Shirley Temple holding American actor, Bill (Bojangles) Robinson's hand in a farmyard during a scene from Edgar Lewis' silent film The Littlest Rebel. *Circa 1932.*
Hulton Archive/Getty Images

Movies at Church

By R.C. McIntyre

Tickets were 10 cents each and were sold on the Jefferson Grade School grounds by fellow students. Hotcakes never went faster. They were movie tickets, but not for movies in a theater. They were sold for the Friday-night movies that were shown every two weeks at the Manito Presbyterian Church on 290th, one block west of Grand Boulevard in Spokane, Wash.

All of this took place around 1929. By then, downtown movie theaters presented talkies, but not the church. Their films came from the silent age, which had just passed.

The church presented them without organ or piano accompaniment. Silent movies required that the audience know how to read. In the early 1920s, schoolchildren learned how to read rapidly and well so they could follow the story at the silent movies.

I don't know what the seating capacity of the church was, but the place was packed for the Friday-night movies as kids of all denominations sat close together in the pews and the choir loft and stood in the aisles. The portable screen was erected in front of the pulpit.

First there was a 15-minute comedy, possibly an early Laurel and Hardy, a Charlie Chase or Lloyd Hamilton picture. Cartoons were never shown. The main movie was usually a Rin Tin Tin feature. Supposedly, "Rinty" had been brought as a puppy from a French World War I battlefield by a soldier who became his owner and trainer. On occasion, his Hollywood rival, Strongheart (also a German shepherd, but lighter in color), would hold forth on the screen. Strongheart was appreciated, but Rin Tin Tin was adored.

Portrait of the canine actor Rin Tin Tin, a German Shepherd, sitting outdoors in a personalized canvas chair, Hollywood, California. Circa 1925. Hulton Archive/Getty Images

All the story lines were similar. Rin Tin Tin or Strongheart was always the hero. Whether they bit off the lighted fuse from the stick of dynamite just before it exploded, jumped onto the empty seat of a runaway stagecoach and grabbed the reins, bringing the horses to a halt, or jumped on the villain's back before he pulled the trigger, they saved the day and the plot. Once the movies started, attention was intense.

In those days it was expected that kids and adults would dress up for any occasion away from home. Overalls and tennis shoes, now called sneakers, were all right for around home or the immediate neighborhood, but for going anywhere else, it was the custom to wear dress clothes. Such was also the case for the Friday-night church movies.

It was unfortunate that I was the only one living in a southeastern direction a mile from the church. Walking along the street at 7 o'clock on a Friday night bound for the 7:30 church movie was no problem. But walking back home alone around 9:30 on a dark, blustery winter evening was another matter. I had to walk through the Manito neighborhood, past the drug store, grocery, library, shoe repair, hardware and service station. All those places had closed by 9 p.m. and all were very dark. In the suburbs, there were only dim street lamps on every other block.

Memories of the just-seen movies inflamed my imagination.

On my way home, if I caught sight of a German shepherd—we called them "police dogs"—I felt relieved, knowing that Rin Tin Tin or Strongheart had sent one of his kind to be my benefactor. Even so, I always ran the last few blocks. ❖

Fudge & Funnies

By Donna Smith

When my brother and I were quite young, we looked forward to Saturday nights for two reasons. The Depression was still on, as was World War II, something we didn't understand or worry about.

After doing our Saturday chores, Rex and I would go to Lake Odessa to help Mom do her weekly shopping. We had a general store in Woodbury, but they didn't carry many things we needed, and their prices were higher than the A&P or the Kroger store in Lake Odessa. At the end of her list, she might order a small bag of Spanish peanuts, and that meant we would be having a special treat.

After packing the groceries and other items into the backseat of the Studebaker, she would drive down Main Street and stop at the Trowbridge Portrait Studio. Trowbridge's also sold the *Chicago Examiner* newspaper.

We bought only the Sunday edition, which came out on Saturday morning. It cost 10 cents, and after we put our dime on the counter, Mrs. Trowbridge wrapped the paper in heavy brown wrapping paper and tied it with heavy butcher twine. We weren't allowed to open the paper till after the supper dishes were washed and put away.

"Shall we make some fudge to go along with the paper?" Mom would ask. Of course, the answer was always yes.

She would measure 2 cups of sugar, 3 tablespoons cocoa, 1 teaspoon vanilla and 1 cup of cream into a white enameled double boiler and set it to cooking on the old wood-burning stove. Rex and I would huddle to the stove as close as possible, inhaling the chocolate smell.

Mom didn't have a candy thermometer, so she used an old-fashioned method of determining if the fudge had cooked long enough. She put a small amount of cold water in a teacup and drizzled a half-teaspoon of hot chocolate fudge into it. She swished the candy around, and if it made a small ball in the bottom of the cup, the fudge had cooked long enough. But if the fudge dissolved in the water, she cooked it a little longer.

Should she not judge it correctly, the candy either refused to harden or became very grainy when it had cooled. Judging the correct consistency was difficult and added a measure of excitement to the whole process.

Staying Warm by the Stove by Charles Berger, House of White Birches nostalgia archives

Then she added the nuts and a teaspoon of butter and beat it for several minutes. The smell was overwhelming and my brother and I would bicker about who got the spoon or the pan.

Mom buttered a small platter and poured the creamy fudge into it. If it was summer, she would put the platter on the cellar floor. If it was winter, she would place it in the snow near the kitchen door.

Dad would unwrap the paper, doling out our favorite sections to each of us. Mom got the women's section, and my brother and I got the comics. Dad took what was left and retired to his chair with his paper and pipe.

My favorite funnies were *Tillie the Toiler, The Katzenjammer Kids* and *Bringing Up Father. Gasoline Alley* made my brother laugh. I knew how to read, so I read to Rex. If I didn't know the words, I made them up—he never knew the difference.

After the fudge had cooled for about 10 minutes, Mom would bring it into the living room. This was the moment of reckoning: Would the candy be cut into pieces, or served with a spoon? ❖

Baseball: A Family Affair

By Helen Bagby

My dad was the consummate baseball fan. As an engineer on the old Wabash Railroad, he often drove a train from our home town in central Missouri to St. Louis. If he had time between trains, he would ride a streetcar to Sportsman's Park to see the Cardinals or the Browns play ball. The next day, with a style and enthusiasm to rival Joe Garagiola, he would report the highlights for his family. Long before I ever saw a game, I had a terrific crush on "Sunny Jim" Bottomley, the Cards' star slugger.

We had the *St. Louis Globe Democrat* delivered to the house every day. I suppose Mom and Dad read the national and international news, and I know we kids enjoyed the funnies, but the real reason for taking the paper was so that Dad could keep up with the two St. Louis baseball teams.

When I was about 12, a new element entered baseball and the whole field of entertainment. Almost overnight, it seemed that we were the only family in town without a radio. Dad was on the fence about buying one. Then my older brother brought the news that baseball games were being broadcast. The next day we had our first radio.

One of my early recollections is of Dad sitting in front of the radio with his eyes closed. Railroading was never a nine-to-five job, and he had probably worked much of the night. Thinking he was asleep, Mom would turn off the radio. Without opening his eyes, Dad would say, "The Cards lead 5 to 3 in the sixth inning. Hornsby is at bat with two on and two out." Confronted with this proof of consciousness, Mom would turn the radio on again.

Later, after we learned to share his enthusiasm, Dad would occasionally take the whole family to a game. Workers in those days had few fringe benefits, but railroad employees were given a pass for the family to ride the train free. One day a week was Ladies' Day at the ballpark, when women and girls were admitted free. We would catch the early morning train for the three-hour ride, spend the rest of the morning window-shopping or sightseeing, go to the ball game in the afternoon and maybe to a movie or vaudeville show in the evening, then catch the last train home. By the time we arrived home we had been gone almost 24 hours, but we were too excited and happy to be tired.

Even with the freebies, our day in the city was expensive for a family of six. Dad chose the games carefully to get our money's worth in excitement. Even in those days almost 60 years ago, the St. Louis Cardinals and the Chicago Cubs already had a solid reputation as the Hatfields and McCoys of baseball. A game between these two teams was our first choice. And if Dizzy Dean happened to be pitching, that was the icing on the cake.

In a close second place was a game between the St. Louis Browns and the New York Yankees. Here the teams were less important than the individual players. No one except my dad expected—or even hoped for—a St. Louis victory. The rest of us wanted to see Babe Ruth hit a long home run.

In those days, St. Louis was aptly described as "First in shoes, first in booze, and last in the American League." This description stuck with the Browns until they sneaked off to Baltimore and changed their name to Orioles. Had my dad been alive when that happened, he would have considered it a personal betrayal.

To us, baseball has always been a family affair. I've enjoyed many a game, in person and on television or radio, with my kids and grandkids, but I'll always be grateful to my dad for introducing me to the sheer pleasure inherent in the shout, "Play ball!" ❖

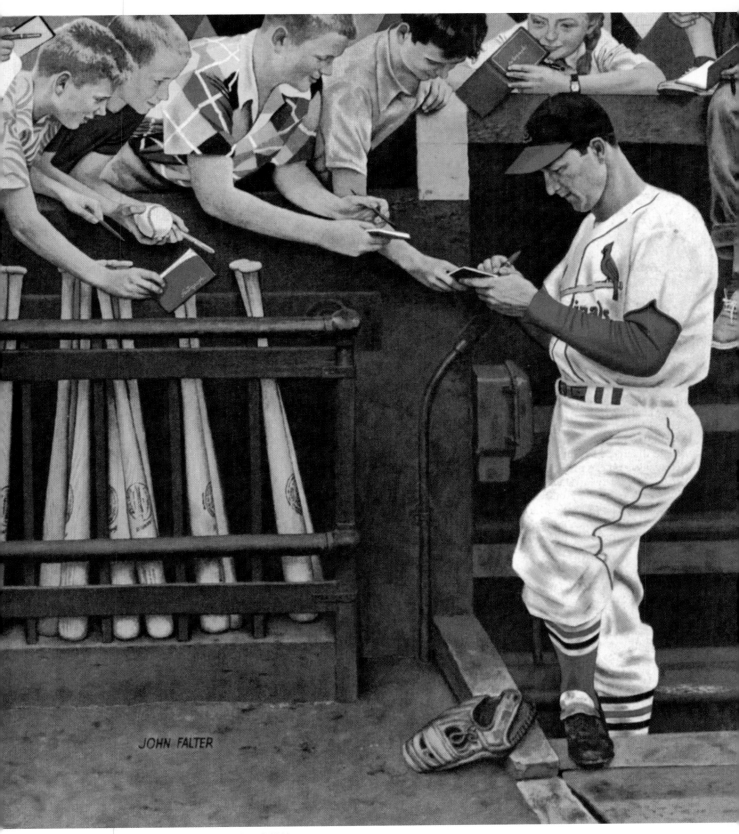

Stan the Man by John Falter © 1954 SEPS: Licensed by Curtis Publishing

Crystal Set Kid

By Joseph Warchol

All too often, a person who wishes to reminisce must be prepared to defend against those who charge that he is suffering a shameful case of nostalgia—a condition usually associated with those who are "out of it," or lost to senility.

I, for one, see no need to apologize, and readily confess that I am prone to countless nostalgia attacks, and I always welcome their warm, friendly glow. I was born near the cooling-off edge of the Roaring '20s (1927), and my memories of the past sustain me in the present.

Some of my favorite memories concern the unbounded joy that accompanied the family's first superheterodyne radio, a second-hand, highly varnished RCA floor model.

Reception depended on a wire aerial stretched outside the length of our housetop. I was awed, unbelieving, to think that the music and voice it produced were pulled magically from the air. I felt certain I was being tricked.

For all its outstanding performance, however, the superheterodyne took second place one day when my older brother Steven built and introduced me to a simple homemade device dubbed "a crystal set." To this day I still marvel at the capabilities of that primitive instrument and my brother's cleverness in devising such a wonder.

True, it could only receive one or two stations, but all the same, we enjoyed many intimate hours of listening pleasure through a single hand-held earphone. Actually, the earphones were part of a double headband set separated so we could both have one to hear the programming.

It was during the Great Depression of the 1930s (of which I was not the least aware) that Steven and I became addicted to the magic that radio transmitted so freely. Night after night we would listen to the new surprises our sets were capable of tuning in. They introduced us to a vast world of music, drama and comedy.

Over the years we built many models of crystal receivers, some utilizing tubes, but I treasure most the early models we assembled out of cigar boxes. An empty cigar box begged from the corner store, a few screws, and a coil made by hand-winding thin insulated copper wire over an empty toilet-paper spool were the basic necessities to get our venture off the ground.

Our expenditures could be counted mainly in time spent. Everything we needed, with the exception of headphones, was scrounged up free-of-charge out of our dad's toolbox. As for obtaining the crystal, I vividly recall one instance when I found a big chunk of it lying atop our wooden fence gate.

Where did it come from? Who placed it there? I have no idea, but I still remain naïve enough to want to believe that there were good fairies back then.

We always worked with dedicated purpose, eager to test our completed efforts. With the cat's whisker attached (made with one of Mom's sewing needles), headphones at the ready and the galena crystal reverently mounted, we were almost operating.

Remarkably, we needed no batteries, nor did we have to plug it into an electrical outlet. All we had to do to get our crystal set to spring to life was attach the aerial wire to a bed spring, and connect the ground lead either to a cold-water pipe or an iron rod driven into the soil outside our bedroom window.

How, then, did it derive operating energy? I know there exists a logical, scientific explanation, but spare me—I still choose to believe the good fairies had a hand in it all.

Today I hear tell of "solid-state electronics." What that means, I do not exactly understand, but would I be far off the mark if I were to assume the crystal set could be considered a solid-state receiver? Instead of vacuum tubes it employed a single galena crystal, which I understand is a lead sulfide mineral. To me it was imbued with both heart and soul—it was alive! Indeed, it was the heart of the system, seemingly reaching out, detecting and gathering into itself a variety of unseen radio frequencies being transmitted through the air.

High-fidelity radio, for all its sophistication, never really impressed me as intimately as the old simple crystal receivers did. Every day after school they provided me with wondrous champions, companions the likes of which are nonexistent today. Hear the roll call: *Jack Armstrong,* truly "the All-American Boy"; *Little Orphan Annie*, a liberated female even before today's concept; *Tom Mix* and *Captain Midnight.*

And I can still recall many of the exciting premiums that were made available to the faithful who purchased a variety of "breakfast of champions" cereals and beverages. There were badges, secret-compartment rings and message decoders. My favorite (from Kellogg's) was a Don Winslow periscope.

My magical galena crystal fired my imagination as I pictured fantastic worlds and adventures that I never could have experienced otherwise. And they all existed within the safe confines of my mind.

Regrettably, television has short-circuited imaginations, for the audience is now made to see exactly what the producers and directors believe they should see. It is a salesman's dream come true—and a viewer's nightmare.

I own my share of reel-to-reel tape and cassette recorders, compact disc players, color televisions, camcorders and VCRs. But I don't hide the fact that I am not enamored of these or many other of today's sleek technologies.

Down deep, I still prefer to be "backward yonder," riding the airwaves with my cigar-box crystal set. ❖

Illustration drawn by Joseph Warchol of his first cigar box crystal set.

AGAIN...Delco-Light contributes

32-VOLT
DELCO RADIO

now offers electric plant owners vastly improved reception... at less trouble and expense

THE DELCO CONSOLE

NO "A" BATTERY ...JUST PLUG IT INTO THE LIGHT SOCKET

Once more the circle of family pleasure widens. The finest music . . . your favorite radio entertainers . . . daily market reports . . . are now brought to country homes with a new degree of clearness and selectivity. Reception is improved amazingly over less modern sets. Your choice of stations and programs is widely increased. And all at a big saving of both operating annoyance and expense!

For the new Delco 32-volt radio operates directly from any individual electric plant circuit. It does away entirely with the recharging nuisance and renewal costs of "A" batteries.

Mail the coupon on opposite page, and ask your Delco-Light dealer to show you this remarkable new set—with tone selector, volume control, 4 screen grid tubes, 2 amazing new Pentode tubes, and large dynamic speaker. Hear with your own ears its truly unusual performance. And remember it's a set of Delco-Light dependability—yours on *generous* terms.

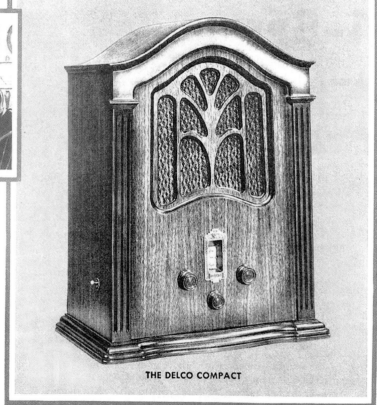

THE DELCO COMPACT

Illustrated at upper left is the Delco Console, a beautifully designed piece of furniture, finished in rich walnut. Delivered to you complete with tubes.

Illustrated above is the handy Delco Compact. Its handsome, walnut-finished case is an addition to the appearance of any room. You can enjoy it now, complete with tubes, at a pleasing price.

★ AND A BETTER BATTERY SET ★

Where no current is available, Delco-Light offers you a new and improved battery set. Its especially designed power battery provides month after month of continuous improved service without thought or attention on the part of anyone. Can you imagine more hours of solid pleasure for the small investment that is needed for this truly *modern* battery-operated radio?

★ ★ THE NEW DELCO RADIOS

Turn Your Radio On

By Ann Oliver

Back in the 1930s and 1940s, radio was our chief means of entertainment. Many great shows amused, inspired and captivated us. Arriving home from school, we could hear the familiar strains of *Little Orphan Annie.*

When we got in the door, we flopped down by the radio to listen to the latest escapades of Annie and her dog, Sandy. In between episodes, we listened to the silver-tongued announcer extol the merits of Ovaltine.

There was also *Jack Armstrong*, "the all-American boy," and "Henry! Henry Aldrich!" And *The Lone Ranger* regularly galloped into our living rooms over the airwaves.

During the day while we were at school or play, Mother listened to her favorite soap operas. She kept a little radio close to the kitchen so she could keep up with *Stella Dallas* and *Ma Perkins* while she cooked.

Nighttime radio was magical. Our spines tingled to the thrillers *Inner Sanctum* and *The Shadow*, and *Lux Radio Theatre* offered really good movies. As trains were so important and so popular in those days, *Grand Central Station* was a huge success.

There were also wonderful musical programs. Who could forget the melodious Bing Crosby crooning his beautiful theme song, *Where the Blue of the Night Meets the Gold of the Day*, or *The Voice of Firestone* and the incomparable Kate Smith? And we loved to listen to *Lucky Strike Hit Parade* every Saturday night.

Radio encouraged us to put our imaginations to work. We all had our own ideas of what our favorite characters looked like, even though we never saw them. Many years later when I was married and we got our first television, one of my favorite radio shows became a television show. I had always had an image of what Mr. District Attorney looked like—and the television character was not it!

Radio showcased some very colorful people back then. I guess the most memorable was W. Lee "Pappy" O'Daniel, the little flower sales-man from Kansas who went to work for Burrus Mills Flour Company in Fort Worth, Texas, and sold Light Crust Flour. He made "Please pass the biscuits, Pappy" a household slogan. His charisma, charm and down-home ways catapult-ed him right into the Texas governor's mansion in the late 1930s, and later the Senate.

Since every housewife made her own bread, flour was a popular commodity in those days, and competition between the brands was stiff. Gladiola Flour sponsored the *Stamps Baxter Quartet*. The show came on at noon as a deep, resonant voice announced, "Time for dinner—and bring on those Gladiola biscuits!" Then the quartet would sing, "The flour that blooms in your oven."

As they came on the air, the Light Crust Doughboys would sing, "We never do brag, we never do boast, we sing our songs from coast to coast. We're the Light Crust Doughboys from Burrus Mills."

I can't talk about radio without mentioning Del Rio, that great broadcasting phenomenon on the Texas-Mexico border. It blasted into every home in America with its 500,000-plus watts. Talk about your colorful characters—it abound-ed with them! Most famous, of course, was Dr. Brinkley with his "goat-gland transplants." And there was Norman Baker, with his nonsurgical cure for cancer.

They shared airtime with countless psy-chics, astrologers, preachers (including one who claimed he could raise the dead) and pitchmen who touted everything from patent medicines to insurance. The Federal Radio Commission and the American Medical Association were constantly after them, but they managed to stay on the air from the 1930s through the 1960s. On the other hand, many a country singer got his start on the station.

The biggest drawback to old-time radio was the static. In town it could be really bad. So when the big championship fight was scheduled to be broadcast, my family made plans to hear it better by going to my sister and brother-in-law's house in the country.

The day of the big fight arrived, and excitement filled the air. Mother cooked up a bunch of food, and we all loaded up and headed to the farm several miles away. When we got there, the women busied themselves in the kitchen while the men rolled Bull Durham cigarettes and had a smoke on the porch.

After supper, it came time to turn on the big battery radio and get the fight. It came in crystal clear, just as they anticipated. We kids were playing in the yard when we heard groans and exclamations of "Oh no!" coming from inside. We ran in to see what had happened. Joe Louis had knocked out his opponent in the first round and the fight was over! We had spent more time getting ready for the fight than the whole contest lasted! But everyone had a good laugh about it and we all enjoyed a visit before we returned to Tyler.

Remember that infamous Halloween night when Orson Welles scared the wits out of millions of people with *War of the Worlds,* his Martian attack story on the radio? Fortunately we had been listening to *Mercury Theater* since the beginning of the broadcast that night, so we knew it was not real. But many others who tuned in late thought we really were under attack from outer space!

It was one of many magical moments—and it could only happen on radio.

That's how it was in the Good Old Days of radio in the 1930s and 1940s. We enjoyed wonderful programs, colorful characters and great music, and our vivid imaginations carried us through it all. Who could ask for anything more? ❖

Cowboy Daydreamer by Don Sherwood, House of White Birches nostalgia archives

Free Television

By Jeff Webb

Back in 1951, when I was 9 years old, television and air conditioning were luxuries many people in my Alabama neighborhood couldn't afford. My family, which included two grandparents and an aunt, wasn't poor, but we came pretty close.

Our sources of home entertainment were a big console radio and an ancient, wind-up Victrola. The records, which belonged to my aunt, were more than 20 years old, one-sided, and featured horrible music. The radio quickly became the number-one attraction in our house.

The hot summer nights down South made everyone search for ways to cool off. In most homes, the heat was relieved only by small electric fans. Real relief usually meant getting out of the house, if only to the front porch.

Lots of folks got out on the streets, bound for nowhere in particular. They just took long walks and passed the time talking with others who were out. Front yards often hosted sort of a round robin as people stopped to chat, moved on, and were replaced by others.

The neighborhood movie theater was a popular destination, since it was air-conditioned! The newsreel, cartoons and feature attraction guaranteed a two or three hours of cool comfort. But that escape was usually just good for one night, since the same program played for a week.

Then there was minor-league baseball. The Birmingham Barons, who played at nearby Rickwood Field, drew big crowds on summer nights. Folks relaxed in the open grandstand, where the air was stirred by old-time ceiling fans hung from the roof. Going to the ball game was something most people could do seven days a week, and many did. When the team left town to play on the road, cooling off at the ballpark wasn't possible.

No matter what they did to beat the heat, everybody eventually ended up home in bed, ready to sleep and dream about the day air conditioning and television would be affordable. Most didn't dream television would make it first.

Just up the street from where I lived there was a small-appliance-and-radio business. It occupied the first floor of a house and the owner and his family lived upstairs. Radios, mixers, toasters and similar items were offered for sale. A collection of these gadgets awaiting repairs cluttered shelves and counters along one wall.

One day, without any notice, a number of television sets were placed on display in the shop's picture window. This brought in lots of folks who examined the sets closely, checked the price tags, watched what was playing for a little while—and left. Everybody wished they had one, but the prices were just out of reach.

After a couple of weeks, some trucks pulled up to the shop and unloaded a bunch of cinder blocks. While folks watched and wondered what was up, workmen laid out rows of blocks in front of the show window. When they were finished, the front yard looked like an outdoor theater because a couple of portable speakers were set up.

Then a banner was hung, inviting everyone to come out, sit and watch television every night, starting at dark, except Sundays, when the sets in the show window were off. Sunday nights were for going to church.

People came—not just from our neighborhood, but from several miles away. They walked, rode bicycles, came on the streetcars and a few even drove their cars. Every night a large crowd watched the free television shows. Chairs, footstools and front-porch furniture were brought by those unwilling to sit on the hard cinder blocks. Families brought babies in strollers and laid down quilts to picnic on. It turned into a six-nights-a-week party, where new friends were made and romances began. The problem of what to do on the sultry summer nights was solved.

I don't know if the owner intended for the free television to be a short-term gimmick to sell sets or if he was just trying to provide some entertainment and a way to beat the heat. Maybe it was both, because suddenly, everybody had to have a television set! And ways would be found to buy them.

I don't really remember how long the free television went on. I remember sitting outside and watching in cold weather because my family still couldn't afford to buy a television. The crowds weren't anything like they had been in the summer because the weather was colder. But a bunch of folks didn't come anymore because they had managed to buy their own television sets.

The great day for me finally came in 1952. I remember it was late spring or early summer because it was hot. My mother and grandfather came in one Saturday morning and announced that they had bought a television set. It would be delivered that afternoon, and our lives, like most

World Series in TV Department by Ben Kimberly Prins © 1958 SEPS: Licensed by Curtis Publishing

of those who had television sets, would be forever changed.

It was amazing how television made you forget how hot it was. Suddenly, the house that had been a steam bath wasn't so bad. After all, if you went out, you would miss Jackie Gleason, Arthur Godfrey, Milton Berle or *Your Hit Parade*. Nobody wanted to do that!

Attendance dropped at the movies and ball games. Not nearly as many people could be found on front porches or visiting anymore, unless they had gotten together for a TV party.

Air conditioning? Well, we managed to get by. Nobody dreamed about air-conditioned homes anymore. They thought about the monthly payment on that television. Heat we could bear. Missing *The Colgate Comedy Hour, The Web* or *Playhouse 90* we could not.

From those early beginnings, television grew into something many people have become wary of. Programming becomes more questionable every year. Despite that, not one but several sets grace most homes. Television has become a baby sitter, and many parents neither know nor care what their children are watching.

Gone are the days when television, like radio before it, was part of the cement that helped keep families together. Those were the Good Old Days. ❖

What Time Is It?

By Donna McGuire Tanner

ecember 27, 1947, is the date recorded in television history as the notable beginning of children's programs.

Radio personality Bob Smith brought his own creation, Howdy Doody, to this new media on NBC-TV *Puppet Playhouse*.

The first Howdy Doody puppet was designed by master puppeteer Frank Paris. He was meant to be a homely country boy, but the stringed fellow was downright frightful.

A short time later the Paris puppet was replaced by the cute, freckled (48 freckles for 48 states), doll-faced, plaid-shirted, all-American Howdy Doody whom a generation of kids grew to love.

Mr. Smith soon donned his trademark fringed suit, and exchanged the "Mr." for the name of his hometown in New York. He was known forever after as Buffalo Bob Smith.

An inner circle of very talented people pulled together to breathe life into the program, which aired Monday through Friday. Included on this list was producer Roger Muir, and a young stagehand, Bob Keeshan, who was the first horn-honking, seltzer-squirting Clarabell the clown. Bob left the program in 1952 and went on to become better known as Captain Kangaroo.

After he left, the role of Clarabell was played by Gil Lamb (1952), Robert Nicholson (1952–1955), and finally by Lew Anderson (1955 to the end of the program).

The show was set in the television town of Doodyville; inhabitants included puppets and humans such as Dilly Dally, Mr. Bluster, Heidi Doody, Grandpa Doody, Flub-A-Dub (eight animals in one), Princess Summerfall Winterspring (first a puppet, then played in turn by actresses Judy Tyler and Gina Genardi) and Captain Scuttlebutt. These characters and Buffalo Bob taught children the wholesome lessons of life. Without realizing it, kids learned how to be a friend, good grooming habits, to go to church, and safety.

The man responsible for building these lessons into the stories and plots of more than 2,000 episodes was writer Edward Kean. He also penned 125 songs, wrote the series of 10 Howdy Doody children's Golden Books, and comic books. And his one-word creation, "Cowabunga," used by Doodyville's Indian Chief Thunderthud, has become a part of modern culture. In any language around the world, this fun exclamation is understood.

The show's rapidly growing popularity led to a market flooded with Howdy Doody toys and products from sponsors including Welch's, Blue Bonnet, Hostess, General Mills Cereals, Mars Candy Company, Royal Gelatin, Poll Parrot Shoes and Tootsie Roll Candy. Howdy Doody items are now collectibles.

Children everywhere wanted to be part of the audience known as the Peanut Gallery. There was a long waiting list for tickets.

In 1955, NBC switched the program to color. This was the same year the show crossed international boundaries with the Canadian version, and the Spanish *Jaudi Daudi* seen in Mexico and Cuba. On Labor Day 1955, *Howdy Doody* changed from a daily format to Saturdays.

On Sept. 24, 1960, Clarabell (Lew Anderson) looked into the camera with quivering lips, and spoke his first on-air words, "Goodbye, boys and girls." The program had ended.

In the 1970s, when Howdy Doody fans reached adulthood, Buffalo Bob was welcomed to colleges and other public appearances. The program was reviewed in 1976 with a different-looking Howdy, but due to this revision and bad time slots, it was cancelled.

In 1987, the 40th-anniversary program was viewed by peanut wannabes all over the country who were hungry to see their childhood heroes once more.

Fifty golden years after *Howdy Doody* first aired, Buffalo Bob and Clarabell (Lew Anderson) were still making live appearances for the children of yesterday, their children and their grandchildren. When Buffalo Bob would ask them, "What time is it, boys and girls?" he would always be greeted with the thunderous reply: "It's Howdy Doody time!"

Buffalo Bob died July 29, 1998, less than a year after the 50th anniversary of the first *Howdy Doody Show*. Thanks for the memories, Buffalo Bob and Howdy Doody. Who wouldn't like to be like you, forever young? ❖

Promotional studio portrait of "Buffalo" Bob Smith with Howdy Doody sitting over his shoulders, from the television series, The Howdy Doody Show. Circa 1948.
Hulton Archive/Getty Images